Segregated

Funds

Segregated Funds

How to Guarantee Your Financial Future

2000 EDITION

Brad Miles

with Michelle Miles

Published in 2000 by Stoddart Publishing Co. Limited
34 Lesmill Road, Toronto, Canada M3B 2T6

Distributed by:
General Distribution Services Ltd.
325 Humber College Boulevard, Toronto, Canada M9W 7C3
Tel. (416) 213-1919   Fax (416) 213-1917
Email customer.service@ccmailgw.genpub.com

04 03 02 01 00   1 2 3 4 5

Canadian Cataloguing in Publication Data

Miles, Brad
Segregated funds: how to guarantee your financial future

2000 ed.
ISBN 0-7737-6102-0

1. Segregated funds.   I. Miles, Michelle.   II. Title.

HG4530.M54   2000   332.63'27   C99-932662-7

Cover Design: Angel Guerra
Text Design: Kinetics Design & Illustration

Printed and bound in Canada

THE CANADA COUNCIL | LE CONSEIL DES ARTS
FOR THE ARTS | DU CANADA
SINCE 1957 | DEPUIS 1957

*We acknowledge for their financial support of our publishing
program the Canada Council, the Ontario Arts Council, and
the Government of Canada through the Book Publishing
Industry Development Program (BPIDP).*

Contents

Acknowledgments

Special thanks are due to my wife Michelle for helping bring the vision to reality, to Gerald Loo for his diligence and ability to keep an eye on all the details, and to all the grandparents for all their help with "the little things."

BRAD MILES

Introduction

Although segregated funds are not a new product, 1998 was the year when this financial wallflower finally made it to the dance floor — and what an entrance!

According to Investor Economics, a consultant to the financial services industry, from 1990 through August 1999 the percentage growth in segregated funds outpaced that of regular mutual funds by more than 500%. During this period, mutual-fund assets in Canada grew from $35 billion to $377 billion, while segregated fund assets grew from $2 billion to $32 billion. This growth rate is expected to continue through 2007. Investor Economics is forecasting an average annual compound growth rate of 17.2% for segregated funds between December 1997 and December 2007, a rate that outpaces their forecast of 11.9% for mutual fund growth over the same period.

This book will help you, the investor, understand the value of making segregated funds a key part of your investment portfolio. With their growth potential and guarantees of principal, segregated funds play a critical role in the development of a successful financial and estate plan.

This 2000 guide to segregated funds is the only source that compares the features of these funds. My competitive review of segregated funds investigates the strength of the insurance carriers, the past performance of their funds, associated costs, different features, and, most importantly, their guarantee of principal. My aim is to help you select the funds best for you. However, I encourage you to consult an investment advisor to ensure your selection of segregated funds is appropriate to your situation.

The book will provide you with:

- a clear understanding of the features and benefits of segregated funds
- two outstanding investment strategies addressing the wealth needs of two types of investors: wealth accumulators and wealth nurturers
- a review of segregated funds in Canada

If you are already familiar with segregated funds, you will find this 2000 guide invaluable in helping you select the combination of segregated funds that is right for you.

So, what's all the fuss about? Segregated funds are a very attractive solution to many of the concerns of the average investor. Let's face it, many investors want the satisfaction of growth through equities or stocks, but also want to be able to sleep at night, without worrying about what the markets are going to do the next day. Segregated funds answer both these needs. They offer growth and security in one neat package. And now that mutual-fund companies are partnering with insurance companies to provide consumers with a wider variety of popular, well-known mutual funds, investors can invest in familiar products through familiar companies.

More specifically, segregated funds offer significant opportunities and benefits for the two stages of investing life. First, they offer investment growth for the wealth-accumulating stage. This stage occurs between 30 and 55 years of age when investors try to accumulate as much wealth as possible for future retirement. Second, they offer growth and security for the wealth-nurturing stage, for investors in retirement who still need some growth for the next 20-plus years, but who also have estate planning needs.

So — welcome to the world of segregated funds!

CHAPTER 1

What Are Segregated Funds?

We've all felt the regret of "if only I'd hung in there." You watch, sickened, as the Dow Jones Industrial Average and the Toronto Stock Exchange Index soar to new heights. Because you were nervous when the stock market sank a few months ago, you moved your equity investment into a Guaranteed Investment Certificate. Now Microsoft and IBM stocks break new "all-time-high records" while your savings bonds slumber away, earning about 4%. You find some comfort in telling yourself over and over that "it could have gone the other way." And you sigh, as you envy those strong-stomached equity warriors who bravely held fast and are now celebrating their climbing fortunes.

Wouldn't it be nice if there was a way to take advantage of stock-market highs without having to endure those painful gut-wrenching lows? A product that would guarantee against market declines, that would let you fly with a safety net?

Segregated funds are precisely that product.

So what are these funds? Many people assume they're like mutual funds, and those people are partly correct. Segregated funds are insurance contracts that offer the potential returns of mutual funds. In essence, segregated funds are mutual funds with a life-insurance policy wrapped around them. With regular mutual funds, the overall value goes up and down with the stock market. With segregated funds, the original value is guaranteed. If the market takes a steep dive, what you put in at the beginning is safe. In addition, many segregated funds have "reset" options, which allow you to lock in your growth as the investments grow. Some people describe them as a "life-insurance mutual fund." (More on this feature below.)

Segregated funds differ from mutual funds in their insurance component, which allows for several unique features. The most notable is that the principal — the amount you put in at the beginning — is guaranteed. This insurance component of segregated funds offers a death benefit, and a maturity benefit as well, after a 10-year maturity period.

Segregated funds receive their name from the fact that insurance companies set aside, or segregate, the funds that are pooled to create a segregated fund. These funds are considered separated, or protected, from creditors and bankruptcy. Segregated funds are not considered part of a company's assets. Thus, in the case of insolvency, they cannot be touched.

When I'm describing segregated funds to people for the first time, I find it easy to use a food metaphor. Think of these funds as apple pie with ice cream. On its own, a slice of apple pie is great, and so is a bowl of ice cream. But put them together, and don't you have a much better dessert? A mutual fund is great on its own, as is insurance, but put mutual funds and insurance together, and you've got a great investment tool.

But some people are just getting used to the thought of mutual funds. Why complicate the matter?

First, let's congratulate all the people who have already purchased mutual funds. They have shown they're committed to getting involved in the markets to grow their money at a better rate than GICs or savings bonds. And the returns on some mutual funds can be very good. However, segregated funds offer tremendous added benefits from a safety and estate planning point of view while maintaining growth similar to, or often as good as, that achieved in mutual funds. Of course, growth depends on several factors, but only segregated funds offer a principal guarantee benefit, and a 10-year maturity benefit, while allowing investors to participate in mutual funds at the same time. Chapter 2 explains in more detail the many benefits of segregated funds.

A Little History

Segregated funds have been around for more than 20 years but only recently have gained attention from investors who love their unique investment features. Their sudden popularity is probably due to a few factors, the most likely being that a key market segment is now ready for the product. Aging baby boomers have been looking for safer havens for their money outside of the lower interest-bearing vehicles such as GICs and the higher, but riskier, mutual funds. Recent market swings have caused concern among these aging baby boomers. No one thought the North American markets could drop between 20% to 30% in the span of a few months as they did in 1998. Although the markets have recovered, particularly in the U.S., this recent experience was a little too frightening for some investors, who feel that their savings may be sizably diminished if left in regular mutual funds or plain old stocks. Segregated funds appeal to investors because they offer growth with security of "investment insurance" in a single package. People work hard to build a nest egg for retirement; they don't like the thought of losing some or all of it.

The group most enthusiastic about segregated funds is the segment of the Canadian population directly ahead of the baby boomers. These wealth-nurturers are aged 55 to 75, and if they're not already retired, they're certainly planning for it. It is estimated that they control $700 billion in financial assets or about 56% of the national total.

Their needs for security and growth are driving the flow of investment money from GIC-type investment instruments and mutual funds to segregated funds. As more people learn about them, segregated funds will probably become just as popular as mutual funds — if not more so because of the unique advantages they offer.

How Do Segregated Funds Perform?

The annual management fee for a segregated fund is usually a little higher than for an ordinary mutual fund in order to pay for the guarantee. Usually it's only a difference of 0.2% to 1.0% more. For that fee, investors not only want insurance and other benefits, but also like to believe the funds are going to perform well. So how does their performance compare to that of regular mutual funds? Performance information can be accessed in a variety of ways: daily newspapers, the Internet, and investment advisors. Before purchasing any type of investment, it is important to investigate its fees and past performance. Although past performance is no indication of future gains, it will indicate to you whether the fund outperformed others in its class or simply didn't do well. Read the fund information folder and the contract closely. As with any investment, stay well informed.

Table 1.1 compares segregated fund returns with mutual-fund returns over one- and three-year periods. As you can see, segregated funds have had similar returns to mutual funds in all asset categories.

Over the last year, segregated funds had a slightly higher

return than mutual funds for U.S. equity and global equity categories. Over the last three years, segregated funds performed similarly to mutual funds in all categories and outpaced regular mutual funds in several equity groups.

Table 1.1
How Segregated Funds Stack Up Against the Competition

Fund Type	Average One-Year Return		Average Three-Year Return	
	Segregated	Non-Segregated	Segregated	Non-Segregated
Asia/Pacific Rim Equity	61 (14)*	55.1 (24)	3.9 (5)	− 3.1 (22)
Asia ex-Japan Equity	(0)	49.7 (10)	(0)	− 5.3 (9)
Canadian Tactical Asset Allocation	9.1 (23)	10.6 (32)	10 (11)	7.6 (25)
Canadian Balanced	10.6 (75)	9.3 (160)	7.8 (50)	8.1 (93)
Canadian Bond	0.9 (60)	0.3 (97)	5.7 (39)	6.6 (79)
Canadian Dividend	8.3 (21)	7.1 (31)	8.5 (2)	10 (28)
Canadian Equity	19 (66)	19.7 (128)	6.9 (32)	9.6 (83)
Canadian High-Income Balanced	12.8 (3)	4.7 (13)	(0)	5.5 (7)
Canadian Large-Cap Equity	19.2 (35)	19.4 (55)	8.5 (18)	9.3 (39)
Canadian Money Market	3.6 (42)	4.2 (103)	3.1 (28)	3.5 (86)
Canadian Mortgage	2.4 (8)	3.3 (17)	4.8 (6)	4.3 (17)
Canadian Short Term Bond	1.4 (6)	2.8 (26)	2.7 (1)	4 (21)
Canadian Small- and Mid-Cap Equity	20.9 (19)	17.4 (83)	5.3 (7)	1.8 (56)
Emerging Markets Equity	36 (7)	33.8 (29)	− 11.3 (2)	− 3 (27)
European Equity	16.2 (12)	12.3 (31)	17.9 (3)	17.4 (26)
Foreign Bond	− 8.2 (14)	− 4.6 (52)	3.5 (9)	4.7 (49)
Foreign Money Market	(0)	3.3 (19)	(0)	4.1 (17)
Global Balanced and Asset Allocation	3.5 (4)	11.5 (47)	5.4 (2)	10.2 (34)
Global Equity	21.1 (27)	24.3 (111)	13.4 (10)	13.2 (72)
Natural Resources	16.2 (5)	20.4 (33)	− 12.2 (2)	− 8.2 (21)
Precious Metals	5.5 (1)	5.7 (18)	(0)	− 21.6 (13)
Science and Technology	52.7 (5)	57.7 (28)	(0)	27.5 (15)
International Equity	29.7 (18)	24.6 (37)	14.1 (8)	11.3 (67)
Japanese Equity	54.8 (1)	74.1 (14)	(0)	6.6 (26)
Latin American Equity	(0)	17.1 (12)	(0)	− 2.4 (11)
North American Equity	17.2 (2)	17.0 (10)	(0)	12.8 (9)
Specialty and Miscellaneous	18.8 (1)	11 (38)	(0)	4.8 (14)
U.S. Equity	23.2 (45)	19 (102)	20 (18)	20.1 (70)

Parentheses indicate the number of funds
(Source: BellCharts, September 30, 1999.)

Table 1.1
How Segregated Funds Stack Up Against the Competition

Fund Type	Average One-Year Return		Average Three-Year Return	
	Segregated	Non-Segregated	Segregated	Non-Segregated
U.S. Small- and Mid-Cap Equity	32.5 (4)	28.1 (26)	(0)	13.2 (18)
Real Estate	10.2 (4)	− 1.1 (10)	8.6 (2)	6 (3)
High-Yield Bond	3.4 (1)	4.9 (13)	(0)	5.6 (8)

Parentheses indicate the number of funds
(Source: BellCharts, September 30, 1999.)

Are Segregated Funds Right for You?

Although segregated funds offer many advantages, they are not
right for everyone. If you need your assets to be liquid, these
funds are not the way to go. Segregated funds are especially well
suited to two groups of people with distinct investment needs.
The first group that will benefit from segregated funds are
investors whose investments are currently residing in conservative vehicles like GICs, but who really need a higher return than
such vehicles offer to maintain their standard of living in retirement or to continue building what they need for retirement.

Segregated funds are a perfect option for these people who
don't want to risk losing any of their investments.

Take my parents, for example. My dad worries about every-
thing, but he's especially concerned that his and my mother's
nest egg might be eroded away or even swept away in a stock-
market fall. They'd love the comfort of knowing that wherever
their finances are invested, the gains they've made can be locked
in and guaranteed. Segregated funds are an ideal product for
them. My parents are representative of wealth nurturers. In
addition to the security that segregated funds offer, and the
quality of its money managers, this group loves the estate features, which will allow them to preserve and pass on their estate
without the usual lengthy procedures and costs associated with
settling a will.

The second group that will benefit from segregated funds are people from 30 to 55 — wealth accumulators. With the way the stock market has been going lately, many younger investors have found their RRSP and investment portfolios have taken a minor, and in some cases even major, plunge. Even though this experience has happened to almost everyone in mutual funds, it's still pretty depressing for anyone getting their RRSP or investment statements in the mail when the markets are down. Segregated funds are a good option for this group simply because of the funds' security aspect, because gains can be locked in to insulate against market declines.

Even more importantly for this group, however, segregated funds are well suited for people who want to significantly grow their investments by "leveraging" or borrowing to invest. Wealth accumulators have more time to establish and benefit from "forced" savings plans, which can yield tremendous financial results by using other people's money to buy segregated funds. This process is explained in Chapter 5.

To understand the many features of segregated funds, read on. The next chapter tells you exactly how you can benefit from these insured investments.

Check the extensive ratings of segregated funds at the back of this book to determine features and performance of specific funds.

Where Do You Get Segregated Funds?

First, segregated funds can be purchased only from insurance companies. However, they can be purchased from those companies through many different channels, including

- life insurance agents
- financial planners
- investment advisors

- stock brokers
- discount brokerages

All investment advisors or financial planners selling segregated funds must have their life-insurance licence and sell the funds on behalf of a life-insurance company.

CHAPTER 2

The Principal and Death Benefit Guarantees, Withdrawals, and the Reset Feature

You may be asking how an investment can possibly guarantee your money. Simply keep in mind that a segregated fund is backed by an insurance guarantee.

Let's say you decide you want to invest $100,000 in a segregated fund. Remember, you've reached a decision about the type of fund or funds you want to participate in with help from your investment advisor. You must purchase segregated funds from a person licensed to sell insurance. Just as with a mutual fund, you complete a purchase agreement and prepare a cheque to purchase the funds. However, with segregated funds, you also fill out an insurance contract and designate an annuitant, the person whose life is insured, and a beneficiary, a person to whom you wish the funds to be disbursed in the event of the annuitant's death. That's it. You've bought yourself a segregated fund.

There may be three or more people involved in a segregated fund.

- *The segregated fund owner* is the person, or legal entity, who has all rights and privileges associated with the segregated fund contract or policy.
- *The annuitant* is the person on whose life the guarantees of the contract are based and upon whose death the death benefit guarantee is payable.
- *The beneficiary* is the person who will receive any amounts payable on the death of the annuitant.

The owner and annuitant must be the same person only for registered contracts such as RRSPs, LIFs, etc. For non-registered contracts the owner may be different than the annuitant. In this book, I have assumed that the owner is the annuitant.

The Principal Guarantee

The principal guarantee of segregated funds works in two ways: as a death benefit and as a maturity benefit.

THE DEATH BENEFIT

Let's look at the death benefit first. If you, as the annuitant, were to pass away, and the markets have gone down since your purchase of the segregated fund, your beneficiaries are guaranteed $100,000, the principal amount you invested (used from the example above). But the markets have gone up and your investments went up as well, your beneficiaries receive the increased market value of the principal. So, if you put $100,000 into a segregated fund, and the portfolio grew to $120,000 at the time of your death, the $120,000 goes directly to your designated beneficiaries.

The death benefit most segregated funds offer is usually a 100% guarantee of your principal investment. A deferred service charge schedule may apply if the segregated fund portfolio value is greater than the death benefit guarantee at the time of death. For more details, see the section on service charges in Chapter 3.

Another good feature of these funds is that your beneficiaries receive the money promptly. The full amount is forwarded quickly, generally within a few weeks of receipt of the death certificate. The value of the fund is determined as of the date of the annuitant's death.

Using segregated funds may result in savings of thousands of dollars in estate and probate fees. For more details on estate planning benefits, see the section on avoiding probate and estate fees later in this chapter.

Many people are curious whether they are required to take some kind of medical or health exam, since segregated funds are a life insurance product. No medical exam is required regardless of your current health status. However, some companies will not allow you to buy the funds after you've reached a certain age, usually 80 or 90 years.

THE MATURITY GUARANTEE

The other key component of the principal guarantee is the maturity guarantee. The Office of the Superintendent for Financial Institutions (OSFI) has mandated that any guarantees of this nature must possess a minimum maturity of 10 years. The maturity date is always 10 years after the date you sign the insurance contract. At the end of the 10-year period, the contract matures, unless you have reset (described below). It is important to note, though, that each time the principal is reset, the 10-year period starts anew. At maturity, which is 10 years after your first deposit, the guarantee covers 100% of your deposits made in that first year. However, if the market value of your deposits is greater than the guaranteed amount, you receive the market value.

Some segregated funds offer a 75% maturity guarantee and there are even some offering a 200% death guarantee. These funds allow resets only on the maturity benefit, and will not reset your death benefit.

The deposits you make into a segregated fund may be made in one lump sum or in continuous deposits. If you decide to make monthly contributions subsequent to the initial deposit, those investments would provide you with a maturity guarantee amount for that policy year. The maturity date for that amount would be from the end of the year, although some companies structure the maturity dates to assign a separate maturity date for each monthly contribution.

For policies that use an annual maturity date, known as the end-of-policy-year date, contributions made the following year would mature one year later than the previous contributions.

A minimum lump-sum amount is required to purchase the funds. A typical minimum investment amount is usually $500 per fund with a possible minimum subsequent purchase of $50 to $100 per month. This will vary depending on the insurance vendor selected. Consult your investment advisor to discuss the restrictions that may apply to these funds.

Once again, let's look at an example using that same $100,000. If you made only one deposit of $100,000 principal, and made no withdrawals, you are guaranteed to receive a minimum of $100,000, no matter how the markets performed, at maturity, or 10 years after the date of deposit or reset. If the market value of your contract has declined to $80,000, you still receive the $100,000 maturity benefit. However, if the market value of this deposit has increased to $200,000, you receive $200,000.

Withdrawals

In the previous section we mentioned making withdrawals from your segregated fund. Unlike locked-in GICs, segregated funds leave your money accessible if you need it. But, think about the big picture. The money you put into segregated funds should have a clear purpose: safety and growth. If you want access to ready cash, set aside a portion of your portfolio in short-term GICs, short-term bonds, or treasury bills.

Investors who put money into segregated funds should do so with a long-term goal in mind, after putting aside additional funds in short-term vehicles such as T-bills or GICs for emergency situations. The money in your segregated fund should not be considered as your emergency cash or slush fund by any stretch of the imagination.

In a real emergency, however, you may have to withdraw some of the money in your segregated fund. In most segregated funds, you may encounter an early-withdrawal fee (ranging, on average, from 6% in the first year down to 0% after the sixth year) if you want to withdraw any amount above the figure allowed by your fund contract. This type of fee is not unusual, since many mutual funds also have this type of early-withdrawal-charge structure. For many segregated funds, the principal withdrawal is limited to 10% per annum, and, should you exceed that amount, a fee may be charged. But let me stress this important point again: If you pull out all or bits and pieces of your principal prior to the 10-year maturity, you receive market value for those funds.

There are two ways in which a withdrawal can be calculated, but one offers more money in your pocket.

Let's say you invested $100,000 in a segregated fund in July 1997, and by January 2000 it has grown to $140,000 in market value. You decide you want to withdraw $5,000. If the segregated fund you are in reduced your principal guarantee proportionately, then your principal guarantee amount is now $95,000, and your maturity guarantee date is still July 2007.

If, however, your segregated fund used a formula to calculate the new guaranteed amount, your new guarantee will be based on the following formula:

Principal	Withdrawal amount	Market value	
$100,000 x	$5,000 /	$145,000	= $3,571.42

The new principal guarantee amount is now $100,000 less $3,571.42, or $96,428.58. The maturity guarantee date is still July 2007. Clearly the formula method favors the investor. Only some funds offer this feature, so read your contract and information folder carefully.

Keep in mind that if you decide to withdraw funds, you could find yourself in a plus or a minus situation with that portion of the fund's principal, depending on how the market is performing when you pull the funds out. If the market value of the fund has increased, so has your principal and the portion you are taking out. But, if the market value of the fund has dropped, the portion you are pulling out is worth less than when you originally invested. Some investors may view this as the downside to segregated funds, but in fact, it is not, if you are using segregated funds as they are intended: as part of a properly balanced portfolio.

If you think about it from the fund or insurance company's perspective, how could any company guarantee principal in the short term, particularly in a market that was turning down, and stay in business? If a company was offering short-term guarantees on funds, everyone would be buying funds from that company, guaranteeing higher prices. Segregated funds are simply not meant to be a short-term investment vehicle.

People who benefit the most from segregated funds are those who have a time horizon of five to 10 years. Once again, this is no different from people who purchase regular mutual funds. Neither mutual funds nor segregated funds promise to make a bundle of money over five years or less, although if your portfolio is quite aggressive, you may be able to do that. Segregated funds are designed to allow you to grow and preserve your investments for use at a later date. In essence, that's why the 10-year maturity benefit is in place.

The Reset Feature

Another very appealing benefit of segregated funds is their reset feature. This feature allows you to reset your initial deposit at higher levels, locking in your growth. Let's look at that initial $100,000 again. Your guarantee at maturity or death would be $100,000, your initial principal. Two years later, your investment has grown to $130,000 and you decide to lock in this gain. You simply notify your financial advisor that you want to "reset" your principal guarantee, and the $130,000 becomes your new guaranteed amount. (Your investment advisor may already be ahead of you on this, and may call you to let you know it's a good time to reset.) That $130,000 is now the amount that you receive upon maturity, or can withdraw from, or that your beneficiaries would receive upon your death.

As with any other investment, you must determine your goals with the assistance of your investment advisor and work together to decide when to reset. The ultimate responsibility lies with you, the investor, to ensure that your finances are being properly managed. You have worked hard for these investments, so you should continue to supervise them.

The speed with which your gains are locked in depends on your financial advisor and the administrative effectiveness of the organization through which you've purchased the segregated funds. How the directive to reset is accepted varies with the provider you choose. Some resets can be accepted verbally by your financial advisor, with the stipulation that a written fax or letter will follow. Some companies will not accept a verbal request but require a fax or letter indicating the directive to reset.

The investor will then get the end-of-day close price on the day the reset request was received. Your advisor should be notified of any reset requests before 4 p.m.

The reset option does, however, have an effect on the date

of maturity. When you reset, you start a new insurance maturity period for your entire policy. Your policy will have a new maturity date that is 10 years after the date the last reset option is used. However, the higher death and principal guarantee benefits are in effect immediately. Many insurance companies limit resetting to two to four times a year. Otherwise, investors would be resetting every day stocks went up.

Let's assume you reset the initial $100,000 at $130,000 two years later. The new principal is now $130,000, and the maturity date is 10 years from the day you exercised that reset option. Another year passes, and the market drops. The actual value of your investment falls to $125,000, but the principal guarantee value is still $130,000 because you reset.

Remember, the reset feature is a part of many, but not all, segregated funds. If you want a fund with a reset feature, ensure that the fund you are considering offers this benefit.

Some investors see the reset feature as a bit of a Catch-22. On the one hand, this feature allows you to lock in growth, but at the same time, it pushes the 10-year maturity date continually out of reach. Remember that the ultimate purpose of the product is to preserve and grow assets. If you wish to access your money in exactly 10 years, choose a segregated fund without a reset feature, or simply choose not to exercise that option. Then, if the markets crash, your principal is guaranteed, and you will receive that amount upon maturity.

Many wealth nurturers apply the reset feature in another way. They purchase the funds, intending simply to grow the pool of money eventually to be forwarded to their beneficiaries. They reset as many times as their policies permit, and pay little attention to what it does to the maturity date. If they need some of the funds, they can usually withdraw 10% per annum without a penalty, depending on when they purchased the funds.

If your objective is strictly growth, use the reset feature to a limited degree, such as for the first five years, and then target a maturity date upon which you intend to use the funds.

In addressing the intricacies of using the reset feature, the most critical starting point is to understand your investment objectives. It is not easy to apply a cookie-cutter approach to any investment strategy since investors' objectives, short- and long-term goals, and resources will always vary. Regardless, always consult an experienced financial advisor to ensure the reset feature is used appropriately to meet your objectives.

Segregated Funds vs. GICs and Mutual Funds: Comparing Tax Treatment, Overall Returns, and Disbursements

The interest you earn on vehicles such as a GIC is considered "interest income" by the government — you are taxed on 100% of your interest income. When segregated stock funds offer cash flow, it is in the form of capital gains, and/or dividend income. You are taxed on only 75% of your capital gains earnings, and you receive a dividend tax credit for dividend income. Therefore, you have a higher after-tax return on your investments. If your investments are outside registered retirement plans, this is certainly more appealing than the 2.25% after-tax return on a 4.5% GIC for someone in a 50% tax bracket.

Segregated funds also compare favorably to mutual funds in the manner in which mutual-fund gains are taxed and distributed. When a mutual fund decides it is time to sell a stock it holds to realize a profit in share price, the investor must pay the capital-gains tax on that profit. The cost of the capital-gains tax is paid by dividing the taxes due among all mutual fund unit holders on a per unit basis, regardless of how long you have been in the fund. For example, if you bought a mutual fund in November, and it decided to declare capital gains in December (this is called a distribution), you are going to be taxed on an increase in share price that you did not participate in. In other words, you'll be taxed on a gain that has taken a year to achieve, although you've been in the fund only a month.

With segregated funds, when a decision is made to sell a specific stock, and realize a profit, it is called an allocation, resulting in a taxable gain or loss of income, which will be reported to you via a T3 slip. "Time-weighted" allocations may be more equitable than mutual-fund distributions because allocations are based proportionally on the amount of units held as well as the number of days they were held throughout the year. Thus a client who purchases 100 units of a segregated fund one week before an allocation would incur less taxable gains than a client who held the same amount of units throughout the entire year. If you may need to take advantage of time-weighted allocations, check that your fund offers this feature. Not all do.

The 100% Foreign-Content Advantage

Because Canada makes up approximately 3% of the world's markets, diversification in U.S. and international markets means more opportunity. In regular registered retirement plans, investors cannot invest more than 20% outside the country. However, with segregated funds, an investor may invest up to 100% in foreign content without any taxation penalties until January 2001. Then the foreign-content restrictions revert to current levels, which is a 1% penalty per month on all registered assets holding 20% or more foreign content. In all likelihood, this restriction level may be moved upward by 2001, since there is growing pressure on the government to increase it.

The 100% foreign-content advantage is a tremendous feature. In spite of the fact that you may be paying more, through fees, for a segregated fund, 100% foreign content permits portfolio gains that recently have not been achievable in the Canadian market. By September 30, 1999, the Toronto Stock Exchange,

Canada's bellwether index, had had year-to-date growth of 7.27%. The Dow Jones Industrial Average had grown 12.5% and the Standard and Poor's Index had grown 4.35% over the same year-to-date period. These types of gains more than compensate for any higher fee charged by segregated funds. Of course, not every year will perform in this way.

Table 2.1
Comparison Chart of the Leading World Indices

		Annual Return (%)		
Year	Canada TSE 300	U.S. Dow Jones Industrial	U.S. S&P 500	Global MS World Index
1999*	7.27	12.50	4.35	5.99
1998	−3.29	17.99	28.34	22.78
1997	15.00	24.78	33.10	14.17
1996	28.30	28.58	22.68	11.72
1995	14.50	36.45	37.12	18.70
1994	−0.20	4.95	1.28	3.35
1993	32.50	16.72	9.92	20.39
1992	−1.40	7.35	7.43	−7.14
1991	12.00	23.93	30.00	16.00
1990	−14.80	−0.58	−3.13	−18.65
1989	21.40	31.71	31.22	14.75

* Year-to-date as of September 30, 1999

Avoiding Probate and Estate Fees

Segregated funds offer probate and estate fee benefits that are particularly attractive to older investors. If you have your investments in segregated funds, and you pass away before the maturity period ends, your beneficiaries receive the greater of the guarantee amount or market value less any withdrawals, bypassing probate and estate fees. The death benefit is received by your beneficiaries relatively quickly, usually within a week after receipt of the death certificate and claim application, and can be paid before the rest of the annuitant's estate is settled.

Unless your investments are set up in a joint account with all your beneficiaries, you cannot do this with regular mutual funds, stocks, bonds, and GICs.

How much are you likely to save by avoiding probate and estate fees? First, probate is a fee paid by the estate of the deceased to the provincial government when a court confirms a will. This process must be undertaken because the government is responsible for ensuring all estates are settled properly.

The amount of probate one must pay is based on the size of your estate, and the fees can be substantial in some provinces. In Ontario, the formula is $5 per $1000 on the first $50,000, and $15 per $1000 on the remainder. Hence, a portfolio of $300,000 is subject to $4,000 in fees payable to the government. This works out to a little over 1%. Probate can be as high as 2% in some provinces.

Probate must be paid before an estate is settled and the proceeds divided. As well, the person who is the executor of the will is entitled to estate fees for handling the process. Estate or legal fees might add another 1–5% to the cost. Using the $300,000 estate mentioned earlier, fees could consume from $3,000 to $15,000. Reducing the probate payable by investing in segregated funds means saving those fees and passing the money directly to your beneficiaries.

The estate planning and probate avoidance benefits of segregated funds, as compared to mutual funds, are another advantage to consider when weighing the slightly higher fees segregated funds may charge.

Potential Creditor Protection

Segregated funds are an insurance product. When your investments are in segregated funds, they cannot be seized by creditors if the beneficiary named is a spouse, common-law spouse, parent, child, or grandchild of the annuitant (the specifications are slightly different in Quebec). This protection is especially beneficial to people who own a business and to those, such as lawyers and doctors, who are exposed to potential legal liability through their professions.

Of course, in certain situations the courts may not allow you to treat segregated funds as a debt "escape hatch." For example, if you moved all your money into segregated funds and then declared bankruptcy the next day, leaving behind outstanding debt, the courts might not look favorably upon you.

Consult your investment advisor to determine if creditor protection could benefit you.

Diversification

Using segregated funds, you can choose from a variety of insurance companies with a variety of types of investment funds; the choices are almost the same as the choices available to you now in mutual funds. Many insurance companies have had their own segregated funds for years, and others are now teaming up with many well-known mutual-fund companies, including BPI, Templeton, C.I., Fidelity, AGF, and Trimark.

Segregated funds are available in Canadian equity funds, U.S. equity funds, bond funds, international equity funds, and money market funds.

This wide range of segregated funds helps investors maintain portfolio diversification. Some people feel that once they retire they need more security, so they move their equity mutual funds into GICs. But then they lose the growth their portfolio needs to maintain their active retirement lifestyle now and in the future. Why not move the mutual funds into segregated funds where you can keep your financial plan going and guarantee it at the same time? It's like having your cake and eating it too!

Diversification means balancing your investments in different asset classes, such as bonds, stocks, and cash. This allows you to get the return you require but with much less risk, because you've spread the risk around. Balance through diversification helps you meet your investment objectives.

It's like planning a balanced diet. For optimal health, you balance your diet with a variety of foods — meat and dairy products, grains, fruits, and veggies. Ultimately, a balanced diet should provide your body with all the nutrition it needs to serve you best. The same theory applies to your investment portfolio. To create a balance of products to make up an investment portfolio, you assign various percentages of your investments to various types of financial instruments. This is your portfolio's "asset mix." A balanced financial diet will include mutual funds, segregated funds, GICs, etc.

Diversification plays a role in two ways — first you choose an asset mix to balance the portfolio, and then within those asset classes, you choose a variety of funds to spread the risk around, thereby reducing overall risk exposure.

With some mutual-fund companies, you can move from one fund to another within a "family" of funds. The same is true with segregated funds. If an insurance company offers six segregated funds including three stock funds, a balanced fund, a bond fund, and one international fund, you can move your money between those funds as often as you want, without any charge. Not that you should do much moving around, though. Once you make a plan, you ought to stick to it. Although you may find it tempting to stray, most investment advisors will recommend you stay committed to the time horizons you've determined.

Your asset mix is determined by lifestyle goals and personal investment objectives. If you experience a major lifestyle change, such as losing your job, receiving a major inheritance, or retiring, consult your investment advisor to determine if your asset mix needs to be reviewed.

If you like a variety of funds, you certainly are not limited to using just one segregated fund investment. You may also hold segregated funds from different insurance companies. That way, you are exposed to a variety of money management styles. The result is increased portfolio diversification, since each fund manager will make different investing decisions.

However, you should be prepared to monitor every fund. Some companies offer funds from many different mutual fund companies under one umbrella. This "fund-on-fund" approach benefits the investor by providing more investment flexibility. For example, Manulife has recently teamed up with a number of mutual-fund companies, such as Fidelity and Trimark, and simply put an insurance wrapper around some of their funds. Consumers can now move between these normally separate companies without the fees they would ordinarily pay outside the Manulife umbrella. The fee for the funds under this umbrella may be slightly higher, to pay for the enhanced range of products and the ability to move between normally separate funds.

Some investors are concerned about the risk of an insurance company going bankrupt and their segregated funds being lost to the company's creditors. It doesn't work this way. In 1994, Confederation Life, a Canadian insurance company, became insolvent. Even so, the investors who owned segregated funds with Confederation Life did not lose their money. The term "segregated" means exactly what it says. When Confederation Life collapsed, those funds were still secure, because they were segregated, insured, and set apart from the company's assets. Confederation Life's segregated funds were picked up and honored by Great West Life. The companies offering segregated funds today are very solid, and now have to pass more stringent financial criteria.

Eligibility for Registered Plans

Many segregated funds are 100% eligible for registered retirement savings plans (RRSPs), locked-in retirement accounts

(LIRAs), registered retirement income funds (RRIFs), and life income funds (LIFs). In segregated funds, as in mutual funds, investors can have the convenience and discipline of investing on a regular basis. You can make deposits monthly, quarterly, semi-annually, or annually through pre-authorized chequing (PAC) plans. The 10-year maturity date begins at the end of the contribution year. The following year's contributions are tallied at the end of that year. Those contributions will have a one-year lag on the previous contributions.

The minimum period for the 10-year maturity guarantee is 10 years from the date of purchase. With some PAC plans, the 10-year guarantee is set at the end of the policy year in which contributions were made. However, other PAC plans will issue a 10-year maturity date from the date of purchase. In addition, some maturity guarantees can be longer (as with Maritime Life). The investor has the ability to set a 15-year guarantee that would lock in a principal guarantee amount after the first five years.

In this scenario there must still be a minimum 10-year guarantee (e.g., from the end of year five to the end of year 15).

Automatic Withdrawal Plans and Foreign-Content Treatment for Registered Plans

If you need access to your funds, you may establish an automatic withdrawal plan, as long as withdrawals fall within the 10%-per-year limit for non-registered plans (20% for registered plans such as LIFs and RRIFs). As mentioned earlier, some early withdrawal penalties may apply.

CHAPTER 3

What's the Catch?

At this point most investors ask, "What's the catch? Why doesn't everyone just switch their mutual funds over to segregated funds?"

Fees for segregated funds tend to be higher than for mutual funds. Just as with a regular mutual fund, an annual fee is charged to oversee the management and administration costs of the fund, called the management expense ratio (MER). Usually this fee ranges from 1.5% to 2.5%. In addition, a segregated fund also charges an insurance fee of approximately 0.4% to 1.0%. The insurance company takes that fee every year for the life of the contract.

So, while you pay 2.0% right now for a regular mutual fund, you'll likely pay anywhere from 0.2% to 1.0% more for a segregated fund, depending on which segregated fund company you choose. However, there are some segregated funds, usually with a lower maturity guarantee, that have annual management fees lower than mutual funds.

Insurance Costs

Determining the cost of the insurance component of segregated funds is difficult, and there will likely be continued debate among actuaries (the people who assist in pricing life insurance products). However, there are several reasons that insurance costs can differ from one type of segregated fund to another.

FUNDS OFFERING 100% GUARANTEES VS. THOSE OFFERING 75% MATURITY GUARANTEES

If a segregated fund has a 100%, 10-year guarantee versus a 75%, 10-year guarantee, the cost of insurance will likely be greater to cover that higher percentage.

EQUITY FUNDS VS. BOND FUNDS

The higher risk and volatility of an equity fund requires a higher insurance cost than a bond fund. Conversely, the underlying investment in a bond fund is so secure that an investor may feel that using a segregated fund to gain exposure to this asset class doesn't make any sense. However, if the investor seeks the segregated fund death benefit guarantee and the accompanying estate planning benefits, a bond fund may be a wise choice.

THE ANNUAL MANAGEMENT FEE

If the underlying annual management fee for a segregated fund is high, the cost of the insurance component of the annual fees will likely be higher. For example, if your segregated fund has an annual management fee of 2.5%, when there is a 100%, 10-year maturity guarantee, the insurance cost, at a minimum, will have to guarantee a 2.5% annual growth in the portfolio.

AGE

Lower age restrictions for the principal guarantee may result in a lower insurance cost. Insurance costs are often higher when older people are allowed to invest in segregated funds, as the probability of paying out the death benefit early in the contract term increases with age. In addition, the likelihood of death before the completion of a 10-year period becomes greater as a person ages. This may result in death benefit guarantee payouts within a short period of time, and possibly in a down market, which represents less overall revenue for the insurance companies.

THE RESET FEATURE

From a cost perspective, it is unclear whether this feature should increase or decrease the cost of insurance. Some actuaries believe that a reset feature can increase the cost of insurance as portfolio growth is locked in. However, it can also be argued that because a new 10-year guarantee period begins again at each reset date, there should not be an increase in the cost of insurance.

Because of the cost of the insurance element, investors are concerned that this cost could be raised at any time by the insurance companies. This is a valid concern. In volatile markets, actuaries are not in complete agreement on what a realistic cost for the life-insurance component of the product might be. Although this discussion may be resolved in the future, some industry experts argue that if there were ever a dramatic rise in the insurance cost, companies might risk losing consumer interest in their product.

Service Charges

When purchasing segregated funds, consider the fees and service charges. Fees are widely considered to be the cost assigned to the client to run the fund on an annual basis, while service charges are generally considered to be the charges you incur to buy the funds initially, such as a front-end load, for example.

Segregated fund costs are similar to many mutual funds. You may pay up to 5% on the initial investment amount (a front-end load sales charge), or you may elect the deferred sales charge (DSC) option. Not all segregated funds offer a front-end option. When you invest using this option and pay a fee up front, you can redeem all or part of your investment at any time with no further sales charges.

In Ontario, each company sets a mandatory sales charge within a specific, non-negotiable range, on all front-end load purchases. Each insurance company determines the amount of that mandatory charge as per their range. In some instances you can negotiate a zero percent front load, depending on the company and their range.

With the more popular deferred sales charge option, you pay a sales charge only if you redeem or surrender your investment during a specified period of time. For example, the segregated fund may have a six-year deferred sales charge schedule. This means you are charged a fee only if you pull your money out during that six-year period. For example, if you surrender all or part of your segregated fund in the first year, you are subject to a 6% sales charge based on the original investment amount. If you surrender all or part of the segregated fund in the second year, the sales charge may be 5.5% of the investment withdrawn. The third year may have a 5% sales charge, the fourth year a 4.5% sales charge, the fifth year a 3.5% sales charge, the sixth year a 1.5% sales charge. In our example, there would be no charges after the six-year period. You can see that the fee for pulling out during a specified period of time goes down each year until it reaches zero. However, most segregated funds will allow you to pull out up to 10% of your investment annually with no sales charge.

Most investors who choose the DSC option are either leveraging the segregated fund over a 10-year time frame, taking advantage of locking in growth on an ongoing basis by resetting the principle guarantee when the portfolio grows, or taking advantage of the estate planning benefits that are offered.

To date, the DSC option remains the most popular with investors, since the investor most likely has a long time horizon (at least five years) to achieve investment growth. From an investment standpoint, a segregated fund is the same as a mutual fund in that you need to be fully invested for five or more years. A longer time horizon increases the opportunity for success.

There are a few no-load options available and with all the recent media attention to DSC charges, these are worth investigating, if they suit your needs. With a no-load option you may invest in segregated funds without paying up front and without having to pay a fee if you pull out early. This option provides you with maximum access to your money at all times, and usually has a slightly higher annual management fee. Although this sounds like a good deal, I recommend that you first ensure that the other product features are meeting your needs.

Regardless of your purchase option, it is important to remember that when you withdraw, or surrender, some of your segregated fund investment, your principal guarantee amount will be reduced to reflect the withdrawal.

Deferred Services Charges and the Death Benefit

Upon death of an annuitant, which I've assumed will be the segregated fund owner, beneficiaries receive a minimum of the principal guaranteed amount. However, with some companies, the DSC schedule may apply if the segregated fund portfolio market value is greater than the death benefit guarantee at the time of death.

For example, if $50,000 was the original principal guarantee amount, and the annuitant died three years later when the portfolio had a market value of $60,000, the DSC schedule might be applicable on the market value. (It is important to note that, upon death, the principal guarantee is always paid out in full.)

Therefore, if a sales charge of 3% applies on early surrender in the third year, the 3% charge may be owed on $60,000, but the beneficiaries will not receive less than the $50,000 principal guarantee. The sales charge would not be applicable on the principal guarantee amount or on the reset amount, only the amount over and above the guarantee amount. This charge varies between fund companies.

The best way to avoid or minimize the DSC charge upon death is to take advantage of the principal guarantee reset feature and reset your segregated fund portfolio each time it grows in value by 3% or 4%, thereby maximizing your death benefit payout. There are many segregated funds that will pay out the greater of the principal death benefit guarantee or market value of the portfolio with no DSC charges.

Another drawback is the fee that may apply if you need to withdraw money from your segregated funds. Whether charges apply and how much they are is often based on how soon you pull out money after opening the segregated fund. Of course, when you withdraw money, you do so at market value.

CHAPTER 4

Why Do I Need the Insurance Component?

When my wife asked me if the insurance component was really necessary, I answered, "Well, look at it this way. We have car insurance. Everyone who owns a home or vacation property buys insurance to protect those properties. My father has boat insurance, and your diamond ring is insured too. You buy health insurance, dental insurance, your credit card gives you new product-purchase insurance, and we insure our income through disability insurance. In fact, we had to purchase out-of-country medical insurance for our vacation in Mexico last year.

"When we pay for house insurance we don't actually believe our house will burn down. However, if it ever did happen, we know we would be given its replacement value. We definitely do not want to lose the equity we've built up in our home over the years. We've worked at least as hard to build up our investments. So why wouldn't we consider insuring them, especially in a scenario where we can lock in any appreciation in value?"

Is a 10-Year Guarantee Necessary?

Although 10 years seems like a long time to invest in a single product, I believe the 10-year guarantee works for both the investor and the product. Consider the current situation in Japan. From the late '70s to the mid-'80s, people idealized and glorified the Japanese economy and way of doing business. Businesses worldwide heralded "Kaizen," the concept of continuous improvement, as the engine of Japanese productivity. North American companies studied Japanese teamwork ideas, and we marveled at their electronics powerhouses and their solid financial institutions. Everyone thought that Japanese quality was the ultimate if you were buying cars or electronic equipment.

Based on all this, Japan's economic performance should have been untouchable. But consider what happened to the Japanese stock market in the last decade. In 1989, the Japanese stock market, the Nikkei, reached a record high of almost 39,000 points, one of the most tremendous stock-market bubbles the financial world has ever seen. Then, it started slipping. By the end of 1990, the Nikkei had fallen to 20,000 points, which was down by almost 50% of its previous high. Over the next two years, it fell to 15,000. Now, it hovers around the 17,700 mark most days.

Many factors contributed to the crushing collapse of the Japanese economy. They include the overall debt load of the nation, foreign ownership of domestic stock while Japanese companies were dumping stock, and poor management in their once-revered financial institutions. Some economists believe that recovery is now in sight. The Japanese government has a plan in place to address the debt problem, and Japanese companies are starting to buy back their stock. The Japanese market is likely to go up again now that their house seems to be getting back in order, but 10 years have passed and the Japanese stock market is still well below its high.

A 10-year principal guarantee would have saved the money of investors who invested in the Japanese stock market 10 years ago. Imagine if your retirement assumptions were based on the market remaining within a reasonable range, and it collapsed by two thirds?

Business people and investors keep trying to anticipate the end of the bull run in North America. No one wants to believe it could collapse like Japan, but in August 1998, many people were very frightened about the North American markets, and the words "recession" and even "depression" were mentioned repeatedly.

While it's very unlikely we could experience something like the Japanese market collapse, the Japanese never thought it would happen to them either. By using segregated funds, you can participate in any market growth, and lock in that growth, while at the same time protecting your investments from any market downturns. The example of the Japanese stock market shows that no one can time the markets. Segregated funds allow you to invest in many of the same stock and dividend type funds that you're in right now, but with a principal guarantee. You don't need to worry about market timing.

CHAPTER 5

Segregated Funds and the Wealth Accumulator: Generating Significant Wealth

OK, so you're convinced that segregated funds can help you grow your investments with security. But you don't know how or where to start.

Begin by finding and talking to an investment advisor about your goals. As an investment advisor myself, I often have the chance to talk to many people about investment planning and strategies for retirement. My role as an advisor is not only to assist my clients in growing their investments, but also to do my utmost to protect their investments from losses. Risk and return represent different things to different clients. Seniors who experience losses do not have the luxury of time to recoup. These losses could seriously affect their style of living. The recent market downturns were evidence that the ever-rising stock market was not without its weak days, and the discomfort people felt was evidenced by the mutual fund sales declines, prompting a return of capital to the safer havens of GICs and Canadian government bonds.

In comparison, my younger clients generally have a different set of needs and concerns. They are wealth accumulators, people trying to maximize their investment growth for future retirement. This group includes investors in the 30- to 55-year-old range who are beginning to plan seriously for retirement. Wealth accumulators frequently express concern about what they can do to significantly increase the amount of money they'll have for the retirement lifestyle they want.

I recently spoke to a couple that is typical of this age group. Karl and Tracy are in their early 40s, and they wanted to be sure they were putting away enough money to retire and afford the lifestyle they desire. As a chartered accountant, Tracy earns a good salary, as does Karl, who owns his own successful small business. They have two children, 8 and 10 years old, they own their home, although they still have a sizable mortgage, and they already maximize their RRSP contributions.

Overall, Karl and Tracy are living pretty comfortably. Their monthly cash flow is good, and in fact, they do have some extra money at the end of each month they'd like to invest. They came to me asking what they should do to better build funds for retirement. I introduced them to leveraging strategies using segregated funds.

First, though, let's commend them for work well done. It's hard work for those in their 30s and 40s to save, pay down a mortgage, raise children, and at the same time contemplate retirement. Karl and Tracy are well ahead of many people in that regard. But, they need some guidance to ensure that their money grows to meet their goals.

I explained to them that segregated funds are a tool they should be considering to help them reach their retirement objectives. Both Karl and Tracy knew a little about segregated funds, but considered them investments for seniors. I explained that there are some very sound economic reasons that wealth accumulators should be jumping at the chance to save and grow their investments using segregated funds.

Equities: The Must-Have Element of Every Portfolio

When talking with people like Tracy and Karl, I often ask them this simple question: "Which investment tool or vehicle will provide the best growth over the next 10 years?"

Most people don't know how to answer the question, or simply answer "mutual funds," which is partly correct. No one ever answers "My house." Why? Because today people rarely see a house as a good investment, or even as an investment. But for many wealth accumulators, homes represent the largest investment they'll ever make, by the simple virtue of the loans and loan interest they pay to finance the purchase.

Most wealth accumulators try to pay off houses the same way their parents did — they put a big chunk of mortgage money in every month, faithfully, and some even pay bi-weekly or weekly to reduce their amortization periods. In general though, paying off a mortgage is a long, slow process.

Why do it that way? Often that's what they've learned from their parents. Their parents' generation firmly believed that paying off your mortgage was one of the most, if not the most, important financial goal to reach, and that's what they taught their children. I'm not knocking that advice. It's good to pay down debt and to own something. But, if you look back 20 years, there was a good reason to buy a home, pay it off, and expect a decent return on that investment.

Twenty-five years ago, the parents of wealth accumulators had either paid off their mortgages or were near that point. At the same time, the first baby boomers were also buying their first homes. This glut of baby boomers were in their 20s and early 30s. They were settling down and needed places to live.

They placed a continuous, growing pressure on the housing market, resulting in a sustained increase in the price of homes. As the baby boomers continued to fuel the demand for homes, their parents saw the value of their homes increase threefold. Anyone who bought a home between 1970 and 1984 was very happy. Values tripled, even quadrupled. Homes were tremendously overvalued. In 1968, my parents bought the house I grew up in for $42,000. In 1990, they sold that home for $238,000, at the peak of the housing boom.

Although most boomers have purchased homes in the cities and suburbs, as they age, their needs will change. The big homes they bought to house growing families won't be needed once their children start leaving the nest. The baby boomers will probably sell their homes and look to buy smaller homes and/or vacation property outside the city in smaller towns. Who will want to buy those big family homes in the city and suburbs?

There is a very small group of home buyers following the baby boomers. They're sometimes called Generation X. They're not a large group compared with the boomers, and even though they will likely settle and buy homes, it is unlikely they will spur any significant demand resulting in growth in city or suburban housing over the next 10 years. In fact, based on supply and demand, there is a strong argument to suggest that prices may even drop over this period. It's bad news for that group of wealth accumulators who say "I'm not worried about retirement. I'll have my house paid off, and I can always sell it and get a smaller home." Sell it, yes, but if few people want to buy it, you'll have less people bidding up the price. So, the $250,000 home you currently own may be worth $270,000 a decade from now. If you sell it, you may still not have enough money for retirement.

So for those of us who bought at the peak of the market, let's say in 1989 when the last of the boomers were frantically searching to get into the market, the prospects for retiring on the growth in the value of homes is not terribly promising.

If we believe that housing prices or residential real-estate equity will likely not grow dramatically over the next 10 years, what's a better investment? The answer: equity in companies. "Equity" is preferable to "stocks" because it illustrates that you are, in a sense, an "owner" of a company.

Start thinking in terms of businesses and companies, for two reasons.

First, look at today's market conditions. Despite the Asian flu that caught the world by surprise in 1998, the conditions for worldwide economic growth remain positive. Analysts believe that an expanded global marketplace and increasing productivity due to continued advancements in technology will combine to create a great climate for business.

Second, think again about supply and demand. Remember our housing market scenario? Well, now that the North American boomer population has finished driving up the value of real-estate equity, they're moving on to stock market equities. Retirement planning is currently becoming critical for this group. The increased savings that come as their children leave home is being channeled into growth investments. This has a positive impact on stock markets. Plus, with 10 years or more as a time horizon, boomers can risk more growth potential than a standard 4.5% GIC.

Relax the House Payments and Borrow to Invest

A wiser choice than buying a home and paying it off may be to synchronize a home mortgage with a segregated fund leveraging strategy. First, arrange the lowest interest rate possible for the mortgage. Then pay it off slowly, making the minimum payments possible, and use the money you're saving every month to leverage. With funds working through a mortgage *and* an investment account, your money will work more effectively for you.

When I advise people to borrow money to invest, they generally aren't keen. When I was talking to Karl and Tracy, I asked Karl how business was when he first started out. He laughed and told me how rough it was, but that they had done well over the long term, and he was pleased by how far they had come. His company was planning a cross-Canada expansion over the next two years, and expected the company's growth of about 10% per annum to contribute well to the company's revenues.

I then asked Karl to think back to the beginning. How was the business started?

He told me that in the beginning they had little spare money. They were lucky to get the initial financing from a bank. He and Tracy sold one of their cars and gave up lots of luxuries like trips and dinners out.

Karl was amazed when I told him he had the makings of a great investor.

It's true, even though Karl knows very little about investing. What did he do right? First, he borrowed money, which is what most people do to build a business. He used someone else's money (the bank's) to invest in his business. Then he continued to borrow, and invest his own time in his business even though it was unprofitable. However, he believed that it eventually would be profitable. And now it is, and will probably be even more profitable over time.

So how does this make Karl a great investor? And, more importantly, how does it tie into segregated fund wealth-generating strategies?

Qualified wealth accumulators may be able to apply Karl's strategy to segregated fund retirement planning. By leveraging — borrowing money to make money — you can build your investments in a more secure, tax-efficient way, resulting in significant wealth.

Segregated funds provide two benefits that both lenders (banks, trust companies, etc.) and investors love: first, a 100%

principal guarantee upon death of the annuitant, and, second, a 100% principal guarantee after 10 years. Put simply, your estate can never lose your principal if you die, and you can never lose your principal over the 10-year period.

One note before we go into the details of leveraging: Leveraging is also suitable for RRSP investments, but it is important to point out that you may not have that much contribution room in your RRSP. Moreover, you cannot deduct the loan interest, which may make leveraging less appealing.

Leveraging

Once you decide that you want to borrow to invest in a segregated fund, the first step is to visit your bank and arrange to borrow funds. The bank will require that you assign or collateralize the segregated fund portfolio with the bank. This means that the bank now has first rights to your investment contract. The insurance contract recognizes your designated beneficiary, but the bank, with first rights to the contract, will forward to your beneficiary what remains after it has taken what it is owed. Assigning your segregated fund portfolio provides you with two very important benefits when you borrow to invest. First, the bank has a much more secure loan on their hands, which makes them more eager to lend to you. Second, it also lets you negotiate the best rate for the loan because it is, in fact, so secure.

In each of the following examples, resetting is not an option.

Assume you've approached a lender and have secured a $50,000 line of credit. The money is to be invested in a segregated fund and the segregated contract has been collateralized with the lender. From here, we can make a few assumptions.

First, let's say that the average rate on your loan for the next 10 years is 8.5%, considering that there are strong reasons for a continued low-interest-rate environment in Canada for some time to come. Now, the $50,000 you invested into a growth-oriented segregated fund is projected to compound at 10% per annum over 10 years, and you are in a 50% income tax bracket. Segregated funds will likely generate income on an annual basis. We have assumed the taxable portion of the portfolio return is 30% (the estimated percentage of the annual segregated fund return that would be taxable as income in each year, e.g., interest, dividends, capital gains). As well, income allocations from the portfolio in our example are taxed at 45% (the estimated tax rate on all income distributions in the segregated fund portfolio with a mix of interest income, dividend, and capital gains. The figure is slightly below the investor's marginal tax rate because dividends and capital gains are taxed more favorably).

Now let's look at your monthly loan payments on that $50,000 loan, assuming the loan will be paid off using a mix of both principal and interest amortized over 10 years. The loan will have a monthly payment of $616.01, for a total payment of $7,392.12 for each year. In this scenario, the interest portion of the payment is higher at the beginning of the loan, and reduces over time. Consequently, the principal portion of the payment is lower at the beginning of the loan, and increases over time. As an example, after the first year, a total of $4,048.24 would have been paid in interest, as compared to the 10th or last year of the loan, wherein the total interest paid is $343.56.

LEVERAGING AND THE DEATH BENEFIT: HOW IT APPLIES

Assume you borrowed $50,000, which you used to purchase a segregated fund, and collateralized the loan in the bank's name. You have arranged with the bank to pay the interest portion only of the loan. After four years, your segregated fund portfolio grew to $73,205, and sadly, you passed away. The bank would receive the $50,000 death benefit guarantee amount, which would pay off the principal amount of the loan. A total of $8,500 in after-tax interest would have been paid to the bank, and a total of $3,132.68 would have been paid in tax on income generated by the investments. Your beneficiaries would receive the remaining $11,572.32 profit. (Remember that there may be loan-application fees and repayment penalties if the loan is paid off early. Check with your lender.)

However, if after four years, for example, your segregated fund portfolio had a market value of $46,000, and you passed away, the bank would still receive the death benefit guarantee of $50,000 to clear the loan. And, even though the value of the portfolio was down to $46,000 at the time of death, your estate owes nothing. (However, you would have made interest payments on the loan for four years, and a small amount of income tax would have been paid for income generated within the funds.) Thus, the insurance provided by segregated funds protects both the investor and lender.

LEVERAGING AND THE PRINCIPAL GUARANTEE: HOW IT APPLIES

Next, let's look at how the principal guarantee maturity benefit would work. Both you and the bank know that after 10 years at minimum, the principal investment is returned. Certainly, the most probable scenario is that your $50,000 is now worth substantially more after 10 years, you're still alive, and you're very pleased. And so is the bank, because the loan will be fully paid off at the end of 10 years, due to the maturity guarantee. From the bank's perspective, this is different from borrowing to invest into private business or real estate where both borrower and the bank have no specific principal guarantees over a set time frame.

Before you run out and try to arrange for a 10-year loan, it's important to point out that it's not quite as simple as it seems. Of course, it would be nice if you could arrange a 10-year loan for a rate you can afford, pay it off over 10 years, then get the principal back, plus any gains made over those years.

But because not all institutions will offer 10-year personal loans, an alternative approach is to obtain a line of credit for the amount you wish to invest and structure automatic monthly loan payments for 10 years. This provides you with a forced savings plan, and you receive your principal plus any gains at the end of the 10-year period.

Remember, because you are collateralizing the segregated fund contract with the bank, you have a secured line of credit or loan. The loan is now backed by the guarantee of returned principal through an insurance contract. The result is a lower interest rate.

Now, let me explain why this is a tax-efficient strategy. You can deduct half of the interest portion of your investment loan payment for tax purposes, assuming you are in a 50% tax bracket. So the real after-tax cost of your annual loan payment is $2,024.12 for the first year of the loan (50% of $4,048.24). The interest rate on your loan is thus not 8.5%, but 4.25%. Consider it free money. By paying more in interest at the beginning of the repayment schedule, you can write off more of your interest in the early part of the loan, which may benefit some investors. Check with your tax advisor.

For interest to be deductible, the investment must produce income. However, capital gains are not considered income. The fund must have the potential to produce dividend and interest income and is not necessarily disqualified simply because it produces capital gains. At the end of 10 years, the total amount of interest paid on the loan would be $23,921.20, or $11,952.79 after tax. In addition, $10,757.76 would have been paid in tax on income and capital gains generated from the segregated funds. Therefore, the net worth of your segregated fund investment after 10 years is $106,976.57. For more details, see Table 5.2 on page 51.

Calculating Principal and Interest Payments for a Loan

The tables on the following pages show principal and interest payments for loans of $100,000, $50,000, $25,000, and $10,000.

For each table, I have assumed the following:

- The investor has a 50% tax bracket.
- The annual return is 10%.
- The loan interest rate, with monthly interest and principal payments, is 8.5%.
- The annual taxable portion of portfolio return is 30%. (This is the estimated percentage of the annual segregated fund return that would be taxable as income in each year, eg. interest, dividends, capital gains.)
- The tax rate on income allocations from portfolio is 45%. (This is the estimated tax rate on all income distributions in the segregated fund portfolio with a mix of interest income, dividend, and capital gains. It is slightly below the investor's marginal tax rate because dividends and capital gains are taxed more favorably.)

Please note that the figures in the following tables and throughout this book are an approximation. Numbers are rounded off to two decimal places, and, therefore, some of the totals may vary slightly.

Table 5.1 $100,000 Borrowed for Investment into a Segregated Fund Portfolio

$1,232.02 Monthly Principal & Interest Payment Amortized over Ten-Years

Year	Beginning of Year Segregated Fund Balance	Annual Fund Return	Taxable Portion of Segregated Fund Return	Income Taxes Payable	Total Annual Payment	Principal Payable Annually	Loan Interest Payable Annually	Loan Interest Payable After Tax	End of Year Segregated Fund Balance
1	$100,000.00	$10,000.00	$3,000.00	$1,350.00	$14,784.24	$6,687.75	$8,096.49	$4,048.25	$110,000.00
2	$110,000.00	$11,000.00	$3,300.00	$1,485.00	$14,784.24	$7,268.71	$7,515.53	$3,757.77	$121,000.00
3	$121,000.00	$12,100.00	$3,630.00	$1,633.50	$14,784.24	$7,900.13	$6,884.11	$3,442.06	$133,100.00
4	$133,100.00	$13,310.00	$3,993.00	$1,796.85	$14,784.24	$8,586.40	$6,197.84	$3,098.92	$146,410.00
5	$146,410.00	$14,641.00	$4,392.30	$1,976.54	$14,784.24	$9,332.28	$5,451.96	$2,725.98	$161,051.00
6	$161,051.00	$16,105.10	$4,831.53	$2,174.19	$14,784.24	$10,140.16	$4,644.08	$2,322.04	$177,156.10
7	$177,156.10	$17,715.61	$5,314.68	$2,391.61	$14,784.24	$11,021.02	$3,763.22	$1,881.61	$194,871.71
8	$194,871.71	$19,487.17	$5,846.15	$2,630.77	$14,784.24	$11,978.39	$2,805.85	$1,402.93	$214,358.88
9	$214,358.88	$21,435.89	$6,430.77	$2,893.84	$14,784.24	$13,018.93	$1,765.31	$882.66	$235,794.77
10	$235,794.77	$23,579.48	$7,073.84	$3,183.23	$14,784.24	$14,098.50	$685.74	$342.87	$259,374.25
Total		$159,374.25	$47,812.27	$21,515.52	$147,842.40	$100,000.00	$47,842.40	$23,905.07	$259,374.25

At the end of the 10-year period:

Your segregated fund portfolio would be worth $259,374.25

Subtract the investment costs:

• The 10-year after-tax loan-interest cost ($23,905.07)

• Taxes payable from income generated by the investment ($21,515.52)

Total net worth of your segregated fund leveraged investment after 10 years $213,953.66

Table 5.2 $50,000 Borrowed for Investment into a Segregated Fund Portfolio

Year	Beginning of Year Segregated Fund Balance	Annual Fund Return	Taxable Portion of Segregated Fund Return	Income Taxes Payable	Total Annual Payment	Principal Payable Annually	Loan Interest Payable Annually	Loan Interest Payable After Tax	End of Year Segregated Fund Balance
					$616.01 Monthly Principal & Interest Payment Amortized over Ten-Years				
1	$50,000.00	$5,000.00	$1,500.00	$675.00	$7,392.12	$3,343.88	$4,048.24	$2,024.12	$55,000.00
2	$55,000.00	$5,500.00	$1,650.00	$742.50	$7,392.12	$3,634.35	$3,757.77	$1,878.89	$60,500.00
3	$60,500.00	$6,050.00	$1,815.00	$816.75	$7,392.12	$3,950.06	$3,442.06	$1,721.03	$66,550.00
4	$66,550.00	$6,655.00	$1,996.50	$898.43	$7,392.12	$4,293.20	$3,098.92	$1,549.46	$73,205.00
5	$73,205.00	$7,320.50	$2,196.15	$988.27	$7,392.12	$4,666.14	$2,725.98	$1,362.99	$80,525.50
6	$80,525.50	$8,052.55	$2,415.77	$1,087.09	$7,392.12	$5,070.12	$2,322.00	$1,161.00	$88,578.05
7	$88,578.05	$8,857.81	$2,657.34	$1,195.80	$7,392.12	$5,510.55	$1,881.57	$940.79	$97,435.86
8	$97,435.86	$9,743.59	$2,923.08	$1,315.38	$7,392.12	$5,989.25	$1,402.87	$701.44	$107,179.44
9	$107,179.44	$10,717.94	$3,215.38	$1,446.92	$7,392.12	$6,509.52	$882.60	$441.30	$117,897.38
10	$117,897.38	$11,789.74	$3,536.92	$1,591.61	$7,392.12	$7,048.56	$343.56	$171.78	$129,687.12
Total		$79,687.12	$23,906.14	$10,757.76	$73,921.20	$50,000.00	$23,921.20	$11,952.79	$129,687.12

At the end of the 10-year period:

Your segregated fund portfolio would be worth: $129,687.12

Subtract the investment costs:

- The 10-year after-tax loan-interest cost ($11,952.79)
- Taxes payable from income generated by the investment ($10,757.76)

Total net worth of your segregated fund leveraged investment after 10 years $106,976.57

Table 5.3 $25,000 Borrowed for Investment into a Segregated Fund Portfolio

$308.01 Monthly Principal & Interest Payment Amortized over Ten-Years

Year	Beginning of Year Segregated Fund Balance	Annual Fund Return	Taxable Portion of Segregated Fund Return	Income Taxes Payable	Total Annual Payment	Principal Payable Annually	Loan Interest Payable Annually	Loan Interest Payable After Tax	End of Year Segregated Fund Balance
1	$25,000.00	$2,500.00	$750.00	$337.50	$3,696.12	$1,672.00	$2,024.12	$1,012.06	$27,500.00
2	$27,500.00	$2,750.00	$825.00	$371.25	$3,696.12	$1,817.24	$1,878.88	$939.44	$30,250.00
3	$30,250.00	$3,025.00	$907.50	$408.38	$3,696.12	$1,975.11	$1,721.01	$860.51	$33,275.00
4	$33,275.00	$3,327.50	$998.25	$449.21	$3,696.12	$2,146.68	$1,549.44	$774.72	$36,602.50
5	$36,602.50	$3,660.25	$1,098.08	$494.13	$3,696.12	$2,333.16	$1,362.96	$681.48	$40,262.75
6	$40,262.75	$4,026.28	$1,207.88	$543.55	$3,696.12	$2,535.12	$1,161.00	$580.50	$44,289.03
7	$44,289.03	$4,428.90	$1,328.67	$597.90	$3,696.12	$2,755.35	$940.77	$470.39	$48,717.93
8	$48,717.93	$4,871.79	$1,461.54	$657.69	$3,696.12	$2,994.70	$701.42	$350.71	$53,589.72
9	$53,589.72	$5,358.97	$1,607.69	$723.46	$3,696.12	$3,254.84	$441.28	$220.64	$58,948.69
10	$58,948.69	$5,894.87	$1,768.46	$795.81	$3,696.12	$3,523.99	$172.13	$86.07	$64,843.56
Total		$39,843.56	$11,953.07	$5,378.88	$36,961.20	$25,000.00	$11,961.20	$5,976.51	

At the end of the 10-year period:

Your segregated fund portfolio would be worth $64,843.56

Subtract the investment costs:

- The 10-year after-tax loan-interest cost ($5,976.51)
- Taxes payable from income generated by the investment ($5,378.88)

Total net worth of your segregated fund leveraged investment after 10 years $53,488.17

Table 5.4 $10,000 Borrowed for Investment into a Segregated Fund Portfolio

Year	Beginning of Year Segregated Fund Balance	Annual Fund Return	Taxable Portion of Segregated Fund Return	Income Taxes Payable	Total Annual Payment	Principal Payable Annually	Loan Interest Payable Annually	Loan Interest Payable After Tax	End of Year Segregated Fund Balance
			$123.20 Monthly Principal & Interest Payment Amortized over Ten-Years						
1	$10,000.00	$1,000.00	$300.00	$135.00	$1,478.40	$668.75	$809.65	$404.83	$11,000.00
2	$11,000.00	$1,100.00	$330.00	$148.50	$1,478.40	$726.84	$751.56	$375.78	$12,100.00
3	$12,100.00	$1,210.00	$363.00	$163.35	$1,478.40	$789.98	$688.42	$344.21	$13,310.00
4	$13,310.00	$1,331.00	$399.30	$179.69	$1,478.40	$858.61	$619.79	$309.90	$14,641.00
5	$14,641.00	$1,464.10	$439.23	$197.65	$1,478.40	$933.19	$545.21	$272.61	$16,105.10
6	$16,105.10	$1,610.51	$483.15	$217.42	$1,478.40	$1,014.05	$464.35	$232.18	$17,715.61
7	$17,715.61	$1,771.56	$531.47	$239.16	$1,478.40	$1,102.14	$376.26	$188.13	$19,487.17
8	$19,487.17	$1,948.72	$584.62	$263.08	$1,478.40	$1,197.88	$280.52	$140.26	$21,435.89
9	$21,435.89	$2,143.59	$643.08	$289.38	$1,478.40	$1,301.94	$176.46	$88.23	$23,579.48
10	$23,579.48	$2,357.95	$707.38	$318.32	$1,478.40	$1,408.99	$69.41	$34.71	$25,937.42
Total		$15,937.42	$4,781.23	$2,151.55	$14,784.00	$10,000.00	$4,784.00	$2,390.82	$25,937.42

At the end of the 10-year period:

Your segregated fund portfolio would be worth $25,937.42

Subtract the investment costs:

- The 10-year after-tax loan-interest cost   ($2,390.82)
- Taxes payable from income generated by the investment   ($2,151.55)

Total net worth of your segregated fund leveraged investment after 10 years $21,395.05

Using segregated funds for more secure leveraging is practical and achievable, and being able to deduct the interest on your loan for tax purposes is a great added benefit. The best benefit of this strategy is that it sets up a forced savings plan for investors. With all the expenses that wealth accumulators have, it may be difficult to set money aside for investing. This way, your money is taken immediately, and you pay yourself first.

Leveraging vs. Paying Off a Mortgage

It is interesting to compare leveraging a segregated fund with the mortgage on your home, because you are already leveraging with your mortgage. You placed a percentage of the home's value down as collateral and borrowed the remainder. The after-tax rate you have for leveraging a segregated fund is lower than most current mortgage rates. Remember, you can't deduct Canadian mortgage interest for tax purposes.

Let's not forget that segregated equity funds will likely grow more in value than your home over the next 10 years. Hence, instead of investing in your home equity, invest in the equity of companies through segregated funds.

When comparing the final costs and returns of paying a mortgage over 10 years with a leveraging strategy, it is important to note that none of the extra expenses associated with home ownership have been included. These costs, as all homeowners find out, can be very expensive. Extra costs to consider include property taxes and maintenance and repair costs, which can be substantial.

$100,000 Mortgage vs. $100,000 Leveraged Using a Segregated Fund

How would paying down a $100,000 mortgage over 10 years compare to borrowing $100,000 for investment for the same 10-year period?

I've made the following assumptions for the leverage strategy:

- The loan is paid monthly with principal and interest payments (amortized like a mortgage).
- The investor has a 50% marginal tax rate.
- The annual return of the investment is 10%.
- The average loan rate for borrowing over the 10-year period is 8.5%.
- Approximately 30% of the segregated fund (income) is taxable at the end of the year.
- The average tax rate for annual income generated from the segregated fund is 45%.

The projected result:

- The monthly loan payment would be $1,232.02 per month.
- At the end of 10 years the loan would be paid off.
- At the end of the 10-year period, the total after-tax interest cost on the loan is $23,905.07.
- At the end of the 10-year period, $21,515.52 has been paid in tax for income generated.
- The segregated fund portfolio is worth $259,374.25 after 10 years.

Therefore, the total net worth of the segregated fund investment after 10 years is:

$259,374.25 − $23,905.07 − $21,515.52 = $213,953.66

Now, let's take a look at the $100,000 mortgage scenario. We can make the following assumptions:

- The mortgage rate for the next 10 years is 7%.
- Payments are made monthly.

- The investor has a 50% marginal tax rate.
- the annual return of residential real estate growth is 2.5% per year.

The projected result:

- The monthly mortgage payment would be $1,155.94 per month.
- At the end of 10 years the mortgage would be paid off.
- The total interest cost for the mortgage is $38,712.80 at the end of 10 years.
- The $100,000 value you have built up in your home has been increasing by 2.5% per annum.

Therefore, at the end of the 10-year period your real-estate equity would be worth $128,008.45. (The 2.5% assumed annual growth rate for residential real estate may in fact be overstated. As the baby boomers begin to sell their homes, the supply of homes will surely exceed the demand, and, therefore, housing prices might actually drop over time.)

AND THE WINNER IS . . .

In conclusion, at the end of the 10-year period, the segregated fund leverage strategy would have provided you with an additional $85,945.21 in equity. Leveraging $100,000 using the segregated fund would translate into a 67% increase in your net worth over borrowing $100,000 for a mortgage!

Using a Line of Credit to Leverage

OK, you say. That sounds good. But I've already purchased a house and I don't think I can afford those extra payments each month. There is an alternative, though, that wealth accumulators can apply, which doesn't use the forced savings concept, but rather takes advantage of the flexible repayment terms of a line of credit. Because a line of credit does not have any structured payments associated with it, you can make a payment whenever you like — any day, every few months, or a big lump-sum payment when you wish. Minimum payment requirements are usually required, similar to those you might have with a credit card. By collateralizing the loan with a principal guarantee, you should be able to negotiate a better interest rate on the line of credit.

Given this fact, here's a different approach to leveraging with segregated funds. Instead of setting up monthly payments for your line of credit that include both the principal-repayment portion and an interest portion, you can arrange to pay off only the interest portion on a monthly basis. Based on the $50,000 secured segregated fund investment, your monthly interest payment would be $354.16 per month, or $177.08 after tax, assuming a 50% tax bracket.

If you follow this disciplined monthly repayment schedule, at the end of 10 years the segregated fund contract matures, and the bank receives its $50,000 principal, which pays off your line of credit. Any profits over and above the $50,000 are yours. So, if we use our assumption of 10% average annual compounded growth, the total portfolio would be worth approximately $129,000 (net of fees) after 10 years with $50,000 going to the bank to pay off the loan principal. When you factor in the after-tax loan cost of $21,250 and the income taxes payable from income generated in the funds, you would have received $47,679.36 in investment profit. You made $47,679.36 after 10 years using the bank's money to invest, and by paying only $177.08 per month in after-tax interest on the loan.

To summarize, wealth accumulators can look at two possible leverage scenarios. Both involve establishing a loan or personal line of credit with a bank. You then use the credit to buy your growth-oriented segregated funds, and collateralize the loan so the bank receives its principal upon death or maturity. Then you have a choice:

- you can choose to pay back both the interest and principal portions of the line of credit on a monthly basis, and take the full value of your segregated fund when it matures in 10 years, since your loan will then be completely paid out then;
- or, you can choose to pay only the interest portion of the loan, and upon maturity, the bank will take the full amount of the principal guarantee, and you will take the profit.

In fact, when you use a personal line of credit in this manner, there are many different ways to design a leveraged segregated fund plan. When you have such flexibility in borrowing to invest, it's hard not to take advantage of it.

There is one final twist to the leveraging strategy. You can make an initial deposit in a segregated fund, collateralize the insurance contract with a bank, and then borrow based on your deposit amount. The amount you can borrow will vary based on the bank and your personal circumstances. However, you may be able to borrow anywhere from one half of your initial deposit up to four times your deposit amount, depending on the lender. Once again, the benefits of leveraging will be available regardless of the amount.

Calculating Interest Payments on a Line of Credit

The tables on the following pages show interest payments over a 10-year period on amounts of $100,000, $50,000, $25,000, and $10,000 borrowed through a line of credit.

Table 5.5 $100,000 Borrowed Through a Line of Credit for Investment into a Segregated Fund Portfolio

Interest Only $708.33 Monthly Payment

Year	Beginning of Year Segregated Fund Balance	Annual Fund Return	Taxable Portion of Segregated Fund Return	Income Taxes Payable	Loan Interest Payable Annually	Loan Interest Payable After Tax	End of Year Segregated Fund Balance
1	$100,000.00	$10,000.00	$3,000.00	$1,350.00	$8,500.00	$4,250.00	$110,000.00
2	$110,000.00	$11,000.00	$3,300.00	$1,485.00	$8,500.00	$4,250.00	$121,000.00
3	$121,000.00	$12,100.00	$3,630.00	$1,633.50	$8,500.00	$4,250.00	$133,100.00
4	$133,100.00	$13,310.00	$3,993.00	$1,796.85	$8,500.00	$4,250.00	$146,410.00
5	$146,410.00	$14,641.00	$4,392.30	$1,976.54	$8,500.00	$4,250.00	$161,051.00
6	$161,051.00	$16,105.10	$4,831.53	$2,174.19	$8,500.00	$4,250.00	$177,156.10
7	$177,156.10	$17,715.61	$5,314.68	$2,391.61	$8,500.00	$4,250.00	$194,871.71
8	$194,871.71	$19,487.17	$5,846.15	$2,630.77	$8,500.00	$4,250.00	$214,358.88
9	$214,358.88	$21,435.89	$6,430.77	$2,893.84	$8,500.00	$4,250.00	$235,794.77
10	$235,794.77	$23,579.48	$7,073.84	$3,183.23	$8,500.00	$4,250.00	$259,374.25
Total		**$159,374.25**	**$47,812.27**	**$21,515.52**	**$85,000.00**	**$42,500.00**	

At the end of the 10-year period:

Your segregated fund portfolio would be worth $259,374.25

The $100,000 loan is repaid in full   ($100,000)

Subtract the investment costs:

• The 10-year after-tax loan-interest cost   ($42,500.00)

• Taxes payable from income generated by the investment   ($21,515.52)

Total net worth of your segregated fund leveraged investment after 10 years $95,358.73

Table 5.6 $50,000 Borrowed Through a Line of Credit for Investment into a Segregated Fund Portfolio

Year	Beginning of Year Segregated Fund Balance	Annual Fund Return	Taxable Portion of Segregated Fund Return	Income Taxes Payable	Loan Interest Payable Annually	Loan Interest Payable After Tax	End of Year Segregated Fund Balance
	Interest Only $354.17 Monthly Payment						
1	$50,000.00	$5,000.00	$1,500.00	$675.00	$4,250.00	$2,125.00	$55,000.00
2	$55,000.00	$5,500.00	$1,650.00	$742.50	$4,250.00	$2,125.00	$60,500.00
3	$60,500.00	$6,050.00	$1,815.00	$816.75	$4,250.00	$2,125.00	$66,550.00
4	$66,550.00	$6,655.00	$1,996.50	$898.43	$4,250.00	$2,125.00	$73,205.00
5	$73,205.00	$7,320.50	$2,196.15	$988.27	$4,250.00	$2,125.00	$80,525.50
6	$80,525.50	$8,052.55	$2,415.77	$1,087.09	$4,250.00	$2,125.00	$88,578.05
7	$88,578.05	$8,857.81	$2,657.34	$1,195.80	$4,250.00	$2,125.00	$97,435.86
8	$97,435.86	$9,743.59	$2,923.08	$1,315.38	$4,250.00	$2,125.00	$107,179.44
9	$107,179.44	$10,717.94	$3,215.38	$1,446.92	$4,250.00	$2,125.00	$117,897.38
10	$117,897.38	$11,789.74	$3,536.92	$1,591.61	$4,250.00	$2,125.00	$129,687.12
Total		$79,687.12	$23,906.14	$10,757.76	$42,500.00	$21,250.00	

At the end of the 10-year period:

Your segregated fund portfolio would be worth — $129,687.12

The $50,000 loan is repaid in full — ($50,000.00)

Subtract the investment costs:

- The 10-year after-tax loan-interest cost — ($21,250.00)
- Taxes payable from income generated by the investment — ($10,757.76)

Total net worth of your segregated fund leveraged investment after 10 years — $47,679.36

Table 5.7 $25,000 Borrowed Through a Line of Credit for Investment into a Segregated Fund Portfolio

Interest Only $177.08 Monthly Payment

Year	Beginning of Year Segregated Fund Balance	Annual Fund Return	Taxable Portion of Segregated Fund Return	Income Taxes Payable	Loan Interest Payable Annually	Loan Interest Payable After Tax	End of Year Segregated Fund Balance
1	$25,000.00	$2,500.00	$750.00	$337.50	$2,125.00	$1,062.50	$27,500.00
2	$27,500.00	$2,750.00	$825.00	$371.25	$2,125.00	$1,062.50	$30,250.00
3	$30,250.00	$3,025.00	$907.50	$408.38	$2,125.00	$1,062.50	$33,275.00
4	$33,275.00	$3,327.50	$998.25	$449.21	$2,125.00	$1,062.50	$36,602.50
5	$36,602.50	$3,660.25	$1,098.08	$494.13	$2,125.00	$1,062.50	$40,262.75
6	$40,262.75	$4,026.28	$1,207.88	$543.55	$2,125.00	$1,062.50	$44,289.03
7	$44,289.03	$4,428.90	$1,328.67	$597.90	$2,125.00	$1,062.50	$48,717.93
8	$48,717.93	$4,871.79	$1,461.54	$657.69	$2,125.00	$1,062.50	$53,589.72
9	$53,589.72	$5,358.97	$1,607.69	$723.46	$2,125.00	$1,062.50	$58,948.69
10	$58,948.69	$5,894.87	$1,768.46	$795.81	$2,125.00	$1,062.50	$64,843.56
Total		$39,843.56	$11,953.07	$5,378.88	$21,250.00	$10,625.00	

At the end of the 10-year period:

Your segregated fund portfolio would be worth	$64,843.56
The $25,000 loan is repaid in full	($25,000.00)
Subtract the investment costs:	
• The 10-year after-tax loan-interest cost	($10,625.00)
• Taxes payable from income generated by the investment	($5,378.88)
Total net worth of your segregated fund leveraged investment after 10 years	$23,839.68

61

Table 5.8 $10,000 Borrowed Through a Line of Credit for Investment into a Segregated Fund Portfolio

Interest Only $70.83 Monthly Payment

Year	Beginning of Year Segregated Fund Balance	Annual Fund Return	Taxable Portion of Segregated Fund Return	Income Taxes Payable	Loan Interest Payable Annually	Loan Interest Payable After Tax	End of Year Segregated Fund Balance
1	$10,000.00	$1,000.00	$300.00	$135.30	$850.00	$425.00	$11,000.00
2	$11,000.00	$1,100.00	$330.00	$148.50	$850.00	$425.00	$12,100.00
3	$12,100.00	$1,210.00	$363.00	$163.35	$850.00	$425.00	$13,310.00
4	$13,310.00	$1,331.00	$399.30	$179.69	$850.00	$425.00	$14,641.00
5	$14,641.00	$1,464.10	$439.23	$197.65	$850.00	$425.00	$16,105.10
6	$16,105.10	$1,610.51	$483.15	$217.42	$850.00	$425.00	$17,715.61
7	$17,715.61	$1,771.56	$531.47	$239.16	$850.00	$425.00	$19,487.17
8	$19,487.17	$1,948.72	$584.62	$263.08	$850.00	$425.00	$21,435.89
9	$21,435.89	$2,143.59	$643.08	$289.38	$850.00	$425.00	$23,579.48
10	$23,579.48	$2,357.95	$707.38	$318.32	$850.00	$425.00	$25,937.42
Total		**$15,937.42**	**$4,781.23**	**$2,151.55**	**$8,500.00**	**$4,250.00**	

At the end of the 10-year period:

Your segregated fund portfolio would be worth $25,937.42

The $10,000 loan is repaid in full ($10,000.00)

Subtract the investment costs:

• The 10-year after-tax loan-interest cost ($4,250.00)

• Taxes payable from income generated by the investment ($2,151.55)

Total net worth of your segregated fund leveraged investment after 10 years $9,535.87

A Word About Market Timing

Another advantage of leveraging is market timing. Of course, sometimes the markets are up, and sometimes the markets are down. Quite frankly, no one knows for sure when these ups and downs will occur. It's during the darkest days of stock-market drops that you have to put on a brave front, and think about investing. When the stock market drops it is usually the best time to invest.

Stock markets are the only "stores" in the world that can have a 30%-off sale, and no one wants to buy anything. Ironically, when the prices are peaking, people are interested and buy.

If you saw a high-quality leather jacket on sale, you would probably rush out to buy it. Now, just imagine that the segregated fund that invests in Microsoft, IBM, CitiGroup, General Electric, Johnson & Johnson, etc., is down 15%. It would make sense to invest in the segregated funds that own those businesses, and to buy when they're on sale.

When I spoke to Tracy and Karl, for example, I asked Karl if he would sell his business because he felt that business might be slower next year, and then buy it back again when the business started to grow. Of course, that wouldn't make any sense. Realize you're investing for the long term.

A final thought: Think with your head and not with your heart. Don't get emotional about investing, particularly when you are leveraging. As if it were your own business, stick to your plan, and don't give up during rough periods. Remember, the stock markets go up and down. Simply let them.

CHAPTER 6

Segregated Funds for the Wealth Nurturer: Growth and Security

The other group of investors whose needs are particularly well suited for segregated funds are those of you in the over-55 age range, whom I have been calling the wealth nurturers. The name is appropriate given that people who fit into this category are attempting to nurture or sustain the investments they've already accumulated. Their main financial concerns involve maintaining asset growth, with an increasing emphasis on preservation of capital, tax reduction, and even estate planning. Wealth nurturers are either about to retire, or are already enjoying retired life.

Segregated funds are powerful tools for this group for several reasons, not the least of which is their ability to provide both growth and guaranteed security, a combination that is almost impossible to find elsewhere.

First, segregated funds offer the potential to continue investment growth, which many nurturers require to maintain their retirement lifestyle. Many wealth nurturers underestimate the income flow they'll need to live, how long they will live, and the amount of money they'll spend. Segregated funds allow wealth nurturers to continue investing in growth-oriented mutual funds with the additional ability to lock in growth through the reset feature. The security of the insurance protects their assets from market downturns and erosion caused by inflation. GICs simply cannot provide these benefits. Thus the maturity and death benefit guarantees protect investments while the mutual fund element provides growth.

Second, segregated funds provide tax benefits that other investment vehicles are unable to offer. Unlike GICs and bonds, whose returns are fully taxed as income (when outside of registered plans, such as RRSPs, RRIFs, etc.), segregated fund stock income is treated as capital gain and/or dividend income. Investors are taxed on only 75% of their capital gains (any money they make on top of the principal), and they may receive a dividend tax credit on dividend income (dividend income is derived from stock dividend payouts made to shareholders from Canadian companies).

Additionally, the estate planning benefits offered through segregated funds are ideal for wealth nurturers. The death benefit guarantee offered through segregated funds assists in simplifying estate planning, reduces the time an executor must spend settling the estate, and directs proceeds quickly and cost effectively to beneficiaries.

In order to fully appreciate the role that segregated funds can play within a wealth nurturer's portfolio, let's first examine some of the issues to be considered as you move into or continue to enjoy retirement.

Maintaining Equity Exposure and Sleeping at Night

In October 1997, stock markets around the world were struck hard with the long-term effects of a lingering economic illness known as the "Asian flu." A global economic slowdown was anticipated by many market analysts, resulting in a common belief that the stock markets would fall. In summer 1998, analysts' fears were realized as the Dow Jones Industrial Average dropped nearly 20%. The TSE Index dropped almost 30%. Everyone talked about a recession, and even a depression, despite the presence of some positive market indicators.

Some investors panicked and sold out their stocks, rather than hanging on for the ride. For these investors, this moderate downturn manifested itself in slumping statements, sleepless nights, and dreams of early or comfortable retirement disappearing. They worried that the nest eggs they worked hard to accumulate were cracking before their eyes, along with their prospects for a comfortable retirement lifestyle.

Admittedly, 1998's downturn was significant. However, it raises some critical points about those wealth nurturers who have invested in company stock or equity mutual funds. First, admire the nurturers who are smart enough to recognize the need for a meaningful equity component in their portfolio. People need more equity or stock exposure in their portfolio than they realize for a couple of reasons, not the least of which is longer life expectancy. If we were to look at the typical 60-year-old today, life expectancy for a man is about another 25 years, and for a woman, perhaps a little more than that. If a couple in their 60s puts most or all of their money into GICs paying out 4.5%, they will not beat or even meet inflation, which is the rate at which your money is eroded over time. Outside a registered plan, even a 5% GIC compounds at only 2.5% after tax in a 50% income tax bracket. It's important to remember the stock market has always, in the long term, outperformed other securities such as bonds, GICs, or T-bills.

Let's assume you have a 50% marginal tax rate and have invested $100,000 in a one-year GIC at 4.5%. The rate of inflation (or the erosion of your money's value) for the year is

2.25%. How would your investment perform at the end of a year?

Table 6.1 GIC Performance over One Year				
Investment Value at Beginning of Year	Annual Income	After-Tax Income	Inflation Cost	End of Year Real Investment Value (after tax & inflation)
$100,000	$4,500	$2,250	($2,250)	$100,000

This scenario illustrates that after tax and minus inflation, the real return on your $100,000 investment is zero.

What is interesting is that if interest rates rise or fall, and the cost of inflation remains half of the annual income return, the net return would remain zero.

People often underestimate the amount of spending they do in their retirement, largely because they're healthier than the average retiree was 20 years ago, and there are more opportunities for travel and hobbies such as golf and entertaining. A couple with combined annual earnings of $100,000 will need about $70,000 annually for a similar retirement lifestyle from all income sources, including RRIFs, LIFs, work pensions, government pensions, etc.

Generally speaking, the typical portfolio of a wealth nurturer lacks the appropriate level of equity exposure to continue investment growth, so that the combination of inflation and increased spending will not result in portfolio erosion. As people move into their 50s and 60s, they often move the bulk of their investment portfolio into conservative investment vehicles, which simply cannot provide the growth they need to avoid such erosion. Wealth nurturers must continue to grow their investments, as they previously did through equity investments. However, wealth nurturers tend to be concerned, understandably, about the possibility of a complete loss if the market crashes.

Instead of staying with conservative GICs, a strategy that erodes your future purchasing power, consider segregated funds the perfect solution. They let you participate in stock-market growth, while allowing you to lock in your growth through the optional reset feature. Segregated funds allow your investments to continue to grow with an insurance "security blanket" protecting your financial future.

Although it is an unlikely scenario, there is a remote possibility that investors may not see any gains in their funds over the 10 years, and, upon maturity, would simply receive their principal returned in full. This could happen if the funds dramatically underperformed, or if there were a general sustained drop in the markets. In this case, those with segregated funds would have lost opportunity by having not participated in other asset classes that might have done better. But remember that such investments might not have provided any gains either.

Wealth nurturers can consider taking out loans, just as the wealth accumulators would, in order to purchase segregated funds (see previous chapter). The only major difference is that wealth nurturers are older, and their time horizon is likely much shorter. That is why the death benefit may be of much greater interest to them. Additionally, their investment objectives will likely be different from those of wealth accumulators, who are generally more growth driven due to their longer time horizons.

CHAPTER 7

Estate and Financial Plans

Assuming their financial planning has been reasonably successful, and they've managed to meet or are on track for meeting the financial goals they've set, wealth nurturers need to build on their plans by making estate planning decisions.

Through estate planning you can decide how you'll preserve those assets you've worked to create, and put processes in place to ensure beneficiaries deal with your assets as efficiently as possible.

Segregated funds assist with estate planning in two important ways.

- When you invest in segregated funds, you sign an insurance contract and name a beneficiary who will quickly receive funds in the case of your (the annuitant's) death.
- The death benefit guarantee is then paid directly to your named beneficiary without probate. Unless your investments are set up in a joint account with all the beneficiaries,

you cannot do this with regular mutual funds, stocks, bonds, and GICs.

Quick and direst payment of the principal guarantee to beneficiaries can be important for two reasons:

First, if you die and do not have a will or an estate plan properly prepared, beneficiaries can find themselves entangled in complicated legal problems. In many cases, individuals who have been named the executor(s) of a will have little or no experience in this area and may struggle with the complications that can arise. Executing a will can be a very time-consuming, complicated task, and it can become very expensive if people do not know what they're doing and must consult a lawyer.

Second, segregated funds are an ideal tool to help avoid probate and estate fees. Probate is a fee charged by the provincial government to ensure the proper settlement of estates. The probate you are charged is based on the size of your estate — up to 2% in some provinces — and it must be paid before the estate can be settled. Potential legal fees could also add another 1–5% to the cost of settlement.

In summary, segregated funds can offer investors an efficient and cost-effective approach to estate planning.

CHAPTER 8

Rating the Segregated Funds

While every investor has distinct investing goals and needs, segregated funds have features and benefits that make them useful, practical tools for both wealth accumulators and wealth nurturers. While critics may argue that the added fees are high, I believe that you get what you pay for. If the added security enables a wealth accumulator to secure a line of credit in order to leverage, the added fee is worth it. If the added fee enables a wealth nurturer to continue growing investment throughout retirement, lock in gains, and find a hobby other than worrying, I'd say again, it is worth it.

It is important that you find the segregated fund that best suits your estate and financial planning needs. I recommend that you speak to an investment advisor for guidance in selection.

The chart on pages 74–75 matches segregated fund features with each of the two strategies the book describes: Generating

Significant Wealth for Wealth Accumulators, the 30- to 55-year-old investor, and Growth and Security for Wealth Nurturers, the 55-plus investor. This chart is intended as a first step toward narrowing down the segregated funds that might be right for your particular strategy. The segregated fund ratings that appear on pages 79–183 provide additional information to aid your selection. Your decision process should take into consideration criteria such as:

- the strength and size of the insurance company
- the professional money managers used
- the specifics of the death benefit
- the specifics of the maturity benefit
- guarantee reset option availability
- purchase options and costs
- management fees
- liquidity and withdrawal criteria
- the number of segregated funds available to choose from in each fund family

Although past performance can never guarantee future returns, I have included the past performance of each segregated fund out of interest.

Table 8.1 Investment Strategy Selector		
Segregated Fund	Generating Significant Wealth for Wealth Accumulators*	Growth and Security for Wealth Nurturers†
AIC Segregated Funds	Yes	Yes – for purchases up to age 90
BPI Legacy Funds	Yes	Yes – for purchases up to age 80
C.I. G.I.F. Funds	Yes	Yes – for purchases up to age 80
C.I. Segregated Funds	Yes	Yes – for purchases up to age 65; if purchased after age 65, the death benefit is 75% and will increase by 5% every year up to 100%

Table 8.1   Investment Strategy Selector

Segregated Fund	Generating Significant Wealth for Wealth Accumulators*	Growth and Security for Wealth Nurturers†
Canada Life	No	Yes — for purchases up to age 80
Canada Life Generations	No (Registered Plans only)	Yes — for purchases up to age 68
Concordia	Yes	Yes — for purchases up to age 80
Co-operators	Yes	Yes — for purchases up to age 75
Cumis Member Funds	Yes	Yes
Empire Life	No	Yes — for purchases before age 65
Great—West Life	No	Yes — for purchases up to age 90
Hartford Life	Yes	Yes — 200% death benefit up to age 70, 100% death benefit after age 70
Imperial Life Millennia	Yes	Yes — for purchases up to age 90
Industrial Alliance	Yes	Yes — for purchases up to age 80
Infinity	Yes	Yes — 200% death benefit up to age 70, 100% death benefit after age 70
London Life Freedom	No	Yes
Mackenzie	Yes	Yes
Manulife GIF Encore	Yes	Yes — up until age 80, 80% guarantee after age 80 regardless of when purchased. The death benefit guarantee amount also increases automatically by 4% every year until contract maturity
Maritime Life	No	Yes — if purchased before age 76
National Life Ultraflex	Yes	Yes — for purchases up to age 65
NNFinancial IMS III	Yes	Yes — 100% up until age 81
North West Life Apex	Yes	Yes
Royal & Sun Alliance	Yes	Yes
Standard Life Ideal Funds	No	Yes
Sun Life SunWise 2000	Yes	Yes — for purchases up to age 80
Talvest Synchrony Funds	Yes	Yes — for purchases up to age 76
Templeton GIF	Yes	Yes — for purchases up to age 80
Transamerica Growsafe	Yes	Yes — for purchases up to age 90
Trimark	Yes	Yes — for purchases up to age 74
Zurich WealthGuard	No	Yes — for purchases up to age 79

* Segregated Fund Strategy for the 30- to 55-year-old investor to generate significant wealth (criteria for borrowing to invest)
† Segregated Fund Strategy for the 55+ investor; growth and security (criteria for 100% Death Benefit Guarantee) —— may vary for registered policies

Note on the ratings

List of Segregated Funds

- AIC Segregated Funds
- BPI Legacy Funds
- C.I. Guaranteed Investment Funds
- C.I. Segregated Funds
- Canada Life Segregated Funds
- Canada Life Generations Funds
- Concordia Investment Funds
- The Co-operators Investment Funds
- CUMIS MemberFunds
- Empire Life Elite Investment Program
- Great-West Life
- Hartford Life Investment Advantage Plus
- Imperial Life Millennia III
- Industrial Alliance Ecoflex
- Infinity Segregated Funds
- London Life Freedom Funds
- Mackenzie Segregated Funds
- Manulife Guaranteed Investment Funds (GIF Encore)
- Maritime Life Segregated Funds
- National Life Ultraflex
- NN Financial IMS III
- North West Life Apex Funds
- Royal & Sun Alliance Segregated Funds
- Standard Life Ideal Investment Funds
- Sun Life SunWise 2000
- Talvest Synchrony Funds

- Templeton Guaranteed Investment Funds
- Transamerica Growsafe
- Trimark Segregated Funds
- Zurich WealthGuard

AIC Segregated Funds

Descriptive Overview of the Insurance Company

Transamerica Life Insurance Company of Canada
Ratings:
A+ (Superior) — A.M. Best & Company
AA+ (Very High) — Duff & Phelps
Passed all eight early warning solvency tests administered by TRAC Insurance Services Ltd.
Assets:
$2 billion, over $75 billion (Cdn) with parent company Transamerica Corp. USA

The Transamerica Life Insurance Company of Canada is the wholly owned subsidiary of Transamerica Corporation USA, one of the world's largest financial service companies. Transamerica Corp. was originally incorporated in 1906 as the Occidental Life Insurance Company and later changed its name in 1942 to the Occidental Life Insurance Company of California.

A federal license in Canada was obtained in 1928 and the company was incorporated in 1970 pursuant to the Canadian and British Insurance Companies Act as Occidental Life Insurance Company of Canada. In 1983, following the lead of its parent company, Occidental became Transamerica Life Insurance Company of Canada.

With more than 90 years of history, Transamerica now operates through more than 6,000 financial advisors and provides a wide range of industry leading insurance and investment products.

Investment Fund Manager
AIC Group of Funds

Death Benefit
Clients have the choice of selecting the level of guarantee in the event of death. The Platinum Guarantee Option provides a 100% guarantee of net original deposits, and the Gold Guarantee Option provides a 75% guarantee. The beneficiary will receive the greatest of the current value of the policy, the value as of the last reset, or the original deposit (less proportionate withdrawals) at the selected guarantee level. The age restriction for both guarantees is age 90 for deposits in non-registered policies, age 69 for registered policies, and age 70 for LIF accounts. Back-end load charges do apply, calculated based on market value.

Maturity Benefit
The maturity period for all policies is 10 years, and/or up to age 100 for all policies (registered and non-registered) except LIRAs, LIFs, and locked-in RSPs, where the maximum age is 80. At maturity, the owner is entitled to receive the current market value, the guarantee amount (selected at 100% or 75% of net original deposits), or the value as of the last reset, whichever is highest. As with the death benefit, the deposit guarantees are subject to age restrictions.

Guarantee Reset Option
Resets are allowed up to two times a year, up to age 90. The owner must notify Transamerica with a signed, written request. Each reset will extend the 10-year maturity period from the date of reset for the entire policy.

Purchase Options and Costs/Automatic Contribution Plan

The maximum age to establish a new contract is age 80 for non-registered policies, age 70 for LIFs, and age 68 for all registered policies. The initial investment must be at least $1,000 ($10,000 for RIFs, LIFs and LRIFs) or $500 per fund. Subsequent deposits, up to age 90, must be a minimum $100, or at least $50 through a pre-authorized contribution (PAC) plan, available on a monthly, quarterly, semi-annual, or annual basis. All deposits made during a given policy year will be deemed to have the same 10-year maturity date.

Deposits and purchases can be made either with a front-end or a back-end load option. The front-end load charge is up to 6.00% of the deposit. The back-end load schedule begins at 6.00% in the first year and declines to 0.00% after six years, and is calculated based on the market value of the policy.

The annual management fee ranges from 2.25% to 2.90%, which consists of the insurance charge (between 0.45% and 0.65% for the Platinum guarantee and 0.25% to 0.35% for the Gold guarantee) and the underlying mutual fund management fee.

Liquidity/Free-Redemption Criteria/Systematic Withdrawal Plan

Partial withdrawals can be made at any time upon request provided that the remaining contract value is at least $750. An automatic withdrawal plan is also available for policies of at least $10,000 that will allow investors to make periodic redemptions of units of funds or to select a surrender amount and the percentage split between funds. These withdrawals will be calculated based on current market values, and will proportionately reduce the death benefit and maturity guarantee amounts.

Owners of back-end load funds may redeem up to 10% of the total units in the contract without any charges (based on current year purchases and units held as of the previous calendar year). This right is not cumulative and cannot be carried forward to future years.

(Source: AIC Segregated Funds, 1999)

Investment Fund Performance

Fund Name	Fund Type	YTD	1 Year	3 Year	5 Year	10 Year
AIC Advantage II	CdnEq	− 16.2	1.0	12.5	−	−
AIC American Advantage	USEqt	− 1.9	24.7	−	−	−
AIC American Inc. Equity	GlBal	− 5.9	− 2.2	−	−	−
AIC Diversified Canada	CdnEq	− 14.0	1.1	15.6	−	−
AIC Income Equity	CaBal	− 5.2	6.1	−	−	−
AIC Money Market	CdnMM	3.1	4.2	3.4	4.0	−
AIC Value	USEqt	− 16.3	− 1.3	12.4	19.4	−
AIC World Advantage	IntEq	1.4	9.3	−	−	−
AIC World Equity	IntEq	− 7.3	14.0	15.4	11.2	−

(Source: BellCharts Inc., as of September 30, 1999)

Because the AIC Segregated Funds were recently launched and do not have a measurable previous track record, the performance of the underlying **mutual funds** without the addition of insurance charges is used.

BPI Legacy Funds

Descriptive Overview of the Insurance Company

Transamerica Life Insurance Company of Canada
Ratings:
A+ (Superior) — A.M. Best & Company
AA+ (Very High) — Duff & Phelps
Passed all eight early warning solvency tests administered by TRAC Insurance Services Ltd.
Assets:
$2 billion, over $75 billion (Cdn) with parent company Transamerica Corp. USA

The Transamerica Life Insurance Company of Canada is the wholly owned subsidiary of Transamerica Corporation USA, one of the world's largest financial service companies. Transamerica Corp. was originally incorporated in 1906 as the Occidental Life Insurance Company and later changed its name in 1942 to the Occidental Life Insurance Company of California.

A federal license in Canada was obtained in 1928 and the company was incorporated in 1970 pursuant to the Canadian and British Insurance Companies Act as Occidental Life Insurance Company of Canada. In 1983, following the lead of its parent company, Occidental became Transamerica Life Insurance Company of Canada.

With more than 90 years of history, Transamerica now operates through more than 6,000 financial advisors and provides a wide range of industry leading insurance and investment products.

Investment Fund Manager
BPI Mutual Funds, BPI Capital Management Corp.

Death Benefit
The beneficiary is guaranteed to receive the greatest of the current value of the policy, the value as of the last reset, or 100% of principal deposits (less proportionate withdrawals), with no age restrictions. Back-end load charges do apply based on market value.

Maturity Benefit
The maturity period for all contracts is 10 years, and the net deposit guarantee (which includes withdrawals) is 100% with no age restrictions. At maturity, the owner is entitled to receive the guaranteed amount, the current market value, or the value as of the last reset, whichever is highest.

Guarantee Reset Option
Resets are allowed up to four times a year, until age 90. The owner must notify Transamerica with a signed, written request. Each reset will extend the 10-year maturity period from the date of reset.

Purchase Options and Costs/Automatic Contribution Plan
The maximum purchase age is 80. For locked-in retirement plans the client must not be over 70 years. The initial investment must be at least $5,000 and the minimum for subsequent amounts is $100 per fund. All deposits made during a policy year will be deemed to have the same maturity date. Deposits can be made monthly, quarterly, semi-annually, or annually through a pre-authorized contribution plan.

Deposits and purchases can be made either with a front-end or a back-end load option. The maximum front-end charge is 5.00% of the total amount received, except for the BPI T-Bill Segregated Fund, where the maximum is 2.00%. The back-end load schedule begins at 6.00% in the first year on the effective date of the applicable deposit and declines to 0.00% after six years, and is calculated based on market value.

The annual management fee, which includes insurance charges above the fee for the underlying BPI mutual fund, ranges from 1.70% to 2.80%.

Liquidity/Free-Redemption Criteria/Systematic Withdrawal Plan

Partial withdrawals can be made at any time upon request. An automatic withdrawal plan is also available that will allow investors to make periodic redemptions of units of funds or to select a surrender amount and the percentage split between funds. These withdrawals will be calculated based on current market values, and will proportionately reduce the death benefit and maturity guarantee amounts.

Owners of back-end load option units may redeem up to 10% per year of the total units in the contract without any charges. This right is not cumulative and cannot be carried forward to future years.

(Source: BPI Legacy Funds, 1999)

Investment Fund Performance						
Fund Name	Fund Type	YTD	1 Year	3 Year	5 Year	10 Year
BPI American Equity Value	USEqt	15.7	49.4	35.1	27.6	18.5
BPI Canadian Bond	CaBnd	− 1.4	0.0	5.4	5.6	7.2
BPI Canadian Equity Value	CdnLC	5.8	18.2	4.9	8.4	7.8
BPI Canadian Mid-Cap	CdnSm	15.9	36.4	−	−	−
BPI Corporate Bond	HiYld	4.6	8.2	−	−	−
BPI Dividend Equity	CdnLC	14.2	26.8	−	−	−
BPI Dividend Income	CaDiv	2.0	6.8	11.2	13.1	9.1
BPI Global Equity Value	GloEq	7.0	29.0	22.0	16.7	13.4
BPI High Income	CaHIn	9.7	14.2	−	−	−
BPI Income and Growth	CaBal	0.6	13.0	−	−	−
BPI Int'l Equity Value	IntEq	5.6	20.3	−	−	−
BPI T-Bill	CdnMM	3.1	4.2	3.7	4.5	6.1

(Source: BellCharts Inc., as of September 30, 1999)

Because the BPI Legacy Funds were recently launched and do not have a measurable previous track record, the performance of the underlying **mutual funds** without the addition of insurance charges is used.

C.I. Guaranteed Investment Funds

Descriptive Overview of the Insurance Company

Transamerica Life Insurance Company of Canada
Ratings:
A+ (Superior)—A.M. Best & Company
AA+ (Very High)—Duff & Phelps
Passed all eight early warning solvency tests administered by TRAC Insurance Services Ltd.
Assets:
$2 billion, over $75 billion (Cdn) with parent company Transamerica Corp. USA

The Transamerica Life Insurance Company of Canada is the wholly owned subsidiary of Transamerica Corporation USA, one of the world's largest financial service companies. Transamerica Corp. was originally incorporated in 1906 as the Occidental Life Insurance Company and later changed its name in 1942 to the Occidental Life Insurance Company of California.

A federal license in Canada was obtained in 1928 and the company was incorporated in 1970 pursuant to the Canadian and British Insurance Companies Act as Occidental Life Insurance Company of Canada. In 1983, following the lead of its parent company, Occidental became Transamerica Life Insurance Company of Canada.

With more than 90 years of history, Transamerica now operates through more than 6,000 financial advisors and provides a wide range of industry leading insurance and investment products.

Investment Fund Manager
C.I. Capital Management

Death Benefit
The beneficiary is guaranteed to receive the greatest of 100% of the original net deposit (which includes withdrawals), the current market value, or the value as of the last reset, less any applicable back-end load charges.

Maturity Benefit
After a minimum 10-year term, investors will receive the Minimum Benefit Amount, which is 100% of the original net deposit, the current market value of the policy at maturity, or the value as of the last guarantee reset, whichever is highest (less withdrawals and fees). Each deposit will have its own maturity date. Policies can be held up to age 100 for non-registered accounts.

Guarantee Reset Option
Investors may choose to lock in their investment gains up to two times per year by resetting the guarantee amount at a higher level. A written request signed by the client is required, and is executed on the fifth day of every month. The maturity term for the entire policy would be extended at each reset for a new 10-year period.

Purchase Options and Costs/Automatic Contribution Plan
The minimum purchase amount is $500 per fund ($1,000 for Money Market), and $100 per fund for subsequent purchases. Non-registered policies may not be issued after the age of 80, and registered policies are subject to current government age restrictions. Contributions are available to clients on an automatic monthly, quarterly, semi-annual, or annual basis, with a set minimum of $50 ($100 for Money Market Fund). Each contribution will have its own maturity period.

The management expense ratio (MER) for each fund is approximately 3.30% including the insurance cost. There is a front-end load option with a sales charge of 5.00%, or a back-end fee option based on a seven-year declining schedule starting at 5.50%.

Liquidity/Free-Redemption Criteria/Systematic Withdrawal Plan

Partial withdrawals, including a systematic withdrawal plan, may be requested and/or set up according to the client's choice of frequency. Regular payments must be at least $100 and the value of the policy must be at least $5,000. An annual allocation of up to 10.00% of the total back-end load option units held may be redeemed by the holder without a sales charge. All withdrawals will proportionately decrease the principal guarantee.

(Source: C.I. Segregated Funds, 1999)

Investment Fund Performance						
Fund Name	Fund Type	YTD	1 Year	3 Year	5 Year	10 Year
C.I. American	USEqt	0.5	12.7	15.9	17.4	–
C.I. American RSP	USEqt	– 1.3	12.9	17.2	–	–
C.I. Canadian Bond	CaBnd	– 1.2	0.9	7.6	9.9	–
C.I. Canadian Income	CaBal	3.1	10.8	7.3	–	–
C.I. Dividend	CaDiv	– 1.1	10.9	–	–	–
C.I. Global Boomernomics RSP	GlBal	4.5	–	–	–	–
C.I. Global Boomernomics Sec	GlBal	8.0	32.0	–	–	–
C.I. Global Equity RSP	GloEq	0.0	18.2	12.1	9.5	–
C.I. Global Sector	GloEq	0.9	18.8	16.4	11.5	11.8
C.I. Harbour	CdnEq	8.3	19.4	–	–	–
C.I. Harbour Growth & Income	CaBal	0.4	7.4	–	–	–
C.I. International Balancd RSP	GlBal	– 2.2	5.8	10.5	–	–
C.I. International Balanced	GlBal	0.7	10.6	13.7	–	–
C.I. Money Market	CdnMM	3.1	4.3	3.6	4.5	–
C.I. Signature Canadian	CdnEq	14.1	–	–	–	–
C.I. Signature Canadian Bal	CaBal	7.0	–	–	–	–
Hansberger Value	GloEq	9.1	23.2	4.2	–	–

(Source: BellCharts Inc., as of September 30, 1999)

Because the C.I. G.I.Fs were recently launched and do not have a measurable previous track record, the performance of the underlying **mutual funds** without the addition of insurance charges is used.

C.I. Segregated Funds

Descriptive Overview of the Insurance Company

Toronto Mutual Life Insurance Company
Ratings:
n/a
Assets:
$134,417 million — Toronto Mutual

The Toronto Mutual Life Insurance Company is a conservative federally chartered company established in 1898.

Investment Fund Manager
C. I. Capital Management

Death Benefit
Upon notification of the death of the annuitant, the beneficiary will receive the greatest of 100% of the original net deposit, the current market value, or the value as of the last reset, less back-end load fees if applicable. The principal guarantee for investors who are age 65 or older starts at 75% in the first year and increases 5% per year on a sliding scale to 100% in five years.

Maturity Benefit
The policy holder will receive 100% of the original deposit (less

withdrawals), the current market value, or the policy value as of the last reset at the end of the 10-year term, whichever is highest. Each deposit will have its own maturity date. Policies can be held up to age 100 for non-registered accounts.

Guarantee Reset Option
Investors may choose to lock in their investment gains up to two times per year by resetting the guarantee amount at a higher level. A written request signed by the client is required, and is executed on the fifth day of every month. The maturity term for the entire policy would be extended at each reset for a new 10-year period.

Purchase Options and Costs/Automatic Contribution Plan
The minimum purchase amount is $500 per fund ($1,000 for Money Market), and $100 per fund for subsequent purchases. Contributions are available to clients on an automatic monthly, quarterly, semi-annual or annual basis, with a set minimum of $50 ($100 for Money Market). Each contribution will have its own maturity period.

The management expense ratio for each fund is approximately 3.30% including the insurance cost. There is a front-end load option with a sales charge of 5.00%, or a back-end fee-option based on a seven-year declining schedule starting at 5.50%.

Liquidity/Free-Redemption Criteria/Systematic Withdrawal Plan
Partial withdrawals, including a systematic withdrawal plan (SWP), may be requested and/or set up according to the client's choice of frequency. Regular payments must be at least $100 and the value of the policy must be at least $5,000. An annual allocation of up to 10.00% of the total back-end load option units held may be redeemed by the holder without a sales charge. All withdrawals will proportionately decrease the principal guarantee.

(Source: C.I. Segregated Funds, 1999)

Investment Fund Performance						
Fund Name	Fund Type	YTD	1 Year	3 Year	5 Year	10 Year
C.I. American	USEqt	0.5	12.7	15.9	17.4	–
C.I. Global	GloEq	1.4	19.8	17.4	12.3	12.3
C.I. Hansberger Value	GloEq	9.1	23.2	4.2	–	–
C.I. Harbour Growth & Inc	CaBal	0.4	7.4	–	–	–
C.I. Harbour	CdnEq	8.3	19.4	–	–	–
C.I. Money Market	CdnMM	3.1	4.3	3.6	4.5	–

(Source: BellCharts Inc., as of September 30, 1999)

Because the C.I. Segregated Funds were recently launched and do not have a measurable previous track record, the performance of the underlying **mutual funds** without the addition of insurance charges is used.

Canada Life Segregated Funds

Descriptive Overview of the Insurance Company

Canada Life Assurance Company
Ratings:
AAA — Duff & Phelps
AA+ — Standard & Poor's
A++ — A.M. Best & Company
Aa2 — Moody's Investor Services
Assets:
Over $30 billion

Since its establishment on August 21, 1847, the Canada Life Assurance Company has provided a broad range of financial products and services for individuals and groups throughout Canada, the United States, the United Kingdom, and Ireland. Canada Life was converted into a mutual life insurance company in 1959, and its core business continues to focus on meeting the needs of clients in the areas of financial security, asset accumulation, and investment management.

Investment Fund Manager
INDAGO Capital Management Inc.

Death Benefit

In the event of the annuitant's death, Canada Life will make a payment to the beneficiary that is the greater of either the current market value of the policy or 100% of all deposits, less any withdrawals. Back-end load fees are not applicable.

Maturity Benefit

Following a period of at least 10 years, the owner of the policy is guaranteed to receive the greater of either the current market value or 75% of net deposits.

Guarantee Reset Option

No resets are available at this time.

Purchase Options and Costs/Automatic Contribution Plan

Non-registered and RRIF/LIF policies may be issued up to age 80. For RRSPs/LIRAs, the maximum age is 68. The initial minimum deposit requirement, excluding RRIF/LIFs, is $1,000 per fund, with subsequent deposit minimums of $500. The RRIF/LIF current minimum deposit is $10,000. Contributions may be made on a regular basis through an automatic system, with a minimum monthly amount of $50 per fund. Subsequent deposits will not affect the maturity term of the contract.

All funds are purchased on a back-end load charge basis. The seven-year schedule begins at 4.50% and declines each year thereafter by 0.50%. The annual management fee ranges from 2.00% to 2.40% per fund.

Liquidity/Free-Redemption Criteria/Systematic Withdrawal Plan

Clients may request a partial withdrawal up to three times per year through written request, provided the policy has a remaining minimum value of $1,000. The third request will be considered at Canada Life's discretion and is subject to a $50 administration charge. RRIF/LIF policy holders are permitted regular withdrawals based on legislated annual minimums without the stipulations mentioned and valued at current market prices.

Clients may also request regular income through the automatic partial withdrawal plan, without triggering back-end load charges, provided there is a minimum of $7,500 when the payments begin. *(Source: Canada Life, 1999)*

Investment Fund Performance						
Fund Name	Fund Type	YTD	1 Year	3 Year	5 Year	10 Year
Canada Life Asia Pacific S-38	AsPac	30.9	61.7	5.2	–	–
Canada Life Cdn Equity S-9	CdnEq	– 1.4	14.5	7.1	9.3	6.4
Canada Life Enhanced Div S-39	CaDiv	– 0.3	8.8	–	–	–
Canada Life Euro Equity S-37	EurEq	– 0.4	21.1	18.4	–	–
Canada Life Fixed Income S-19	CaBnd	– 1.4	– 0.1	6.0	8.0	8.4
Canada Life Int'l Bond S-36	FgnBd	– 10.8	– 9.2	5.7	7.4	–
Canada Life Managed S-35	CaBal	– 1.1	8.5	7.5	9.4	8.0
Canada Life Money Market S-29	CdnMM	2.6	3.6	3.1	3.9	5.6
Canada Life US & Int'l Eq S-34	GloEq	0.3	21.9	16.9	16.2	14.1

(Source: BellCharts Inc., as of September 30, 1999)

Canada Life Generations Funds

(for registered accounts only — RSPs, RIFs, LIFs, LIRAs)

Descriptive Overview of the Insurance Company

Canada Life Assurance Company
Ratings:
AAA — Duff & Phelps
AA+ — Standard & Poor's
A++ — A.M. Best & Company
Aa2 — Moody's Investor Services
Assets:
Over $30 billion

Since its establishment on August 21, 1847, the Canada Life Assurance Company has provided a broad range of financial products and services for individuals and groups throughout Canada, the United States, the United Kingdom, and Ireland. Canada Life was converted into a mutual life insurance company in 1959, and its core business continues to focus on meeting the needs of clients in the areas of financial security, asset accumulation, and investment management.

Investment Fund Managers
AGF Funds Inc.
AIC Group of Funds

Bissett & Associates Investment Management Ltd.
C.I. Mutual Funds
Fidelity Investments Canada Ltd.
INDAGO Capital Management Inc.
Scudder, Stevens and Clark of Canada Ltd.
TDQC (Toronto Dominion Quantitative Capital)
Templeton Management Inc.
Trimark Investments Management Inc.

Death Benefit

Upon notification of the annuitant's death, the beneficiary will receive from Canada Life a payment that is the greatest of the current market value of the policy, the value as of the last reset, or 100% of all deposits, less any withdrawals. Any back-end load charges are not applicable.

Maturity Benefit

After a period of 10 years from the date of deposit or the date of last reset, the owner of the policy is guaranteed to receive the current market value, 75% of net original deposits, or the value as of the last reset, whichever is highest.

Guarantee Reset Option

Clients may reset their policies up to two times per contract year. When a reset is done, all existing deposit maturity dates will be changed to a new maturity date that is 10 years from the date of reset, and the death benefit and maturity guarantees will be based on the new reset amount.

Purchase Options and Costs/Automatic Contribution Plan

Both registered and non-registered policies are available for purchase up to age 68 and age 80, respectively. The initial minimum deposit required is a $1,000 lump sum deposit, or $50 with a monthly automatic contribution of at least $50. Each subsequent deposit of a minimum $50 will have its own maturity date until the client resets the policy.

All funds are purchased on a back-end load charge basis. The eight-year schedule begins at 4.50% and declines each year thereafter by 0.50%. The annual management fee ranges from 2.00% for bond funds to 3.85% for global equity funds.

Liquidity/Free-Redemption Criteria/Systematic Withdrawal Plan
Clients may request a full or partial withdrawal at any time, subject to any applicable back-end load charges and administration costs. An annual allocation of up to 10.00% of the market value of each fund, as calculated at the end of the previous calendar year, may be withdrawn without incurring any back-end load charges. Withdrawals must be a minimum of $500, and all values will be based on the current market value. RRIF/LIFs are permitted regular withdrawals based on legislated annual minimums and valued at current market prices.
(Source: Canada Life, 1999)

Investment Fund Performance						
Fund Name	Fund Type	YTD	1 Year	3 Year	5 Year	10 Year
AGF Canadian Bond	Bond	− 1.8	− 0.6	6.8	9.2	9.3
AGF Dividend	Divid	− 1.2	8.7	13.5	14.2	10.7
AIC Diversified Canada	CanEq	− 14.0	1.1	15.6	−	−
AIC Value	USEq	− 16.3	− 1.3	12.4	19.4	−
AIC World Equity	GloEq	− 7.3	14.0	15.4	11.2	−
Bissett Bond	Bond	− 1.5	0.1	7.1	9.6	9.4
Bissett Canadian Equity	CanEq	− 3.4	10.1	12.1	15.0	11.5
Bissett Retirement	Balnc	− 1.6	7.1	10.4	12.8	−
Bissett Small Cap	SmCap	− 4.5	3.1	0.9	8.4	−
C.I. Global Boomernomics Sectr	Spec	8.0	32.0	−	−	−
C.I. Global Equity RSP	GloEq	0.0	18.2	12.1	9.5	−
C.I. Harbour	CanEq	8.3	19.4	−	−	−
C.I. Harbour Growth and Income	Balnc	0.4	7.4	−	−	−
Canada Life Cdn Equity S-9	CanEq	− 1.4	14.5	7.1	9.3	6.4
Canada Life Enhanced Div S-39	Divid	− 0.3	8.8	−	−	−
Canada Life Euro Equity S-37	Europ	− 0.4	21.1	18.4	−	−

Investment Fund Performance

Fund Name	Fund Type	YTD	1 Year	3 Year	5 Year	10 Year
Canada Life Fixed Income S-19	Bond	– 1.4	– 0.1	6.0	8.0	8.4
Canada Life Int'l Bond S-36	IntBd	– 10.8	– 9.2	5.7	7.4	–
Canada Life Managed S-35	Balnc	– 1.1	8.5	7.5	9.4	8.0
Canada Life Money Market S-29	CanMM	2.6	3.6	3.1	3.9	5.6
Canada Life US & Int'l Eq S-34	GloEq	0.3	21.9	16.9	16.2	14.1
Fidelity Cdn Asset Allocation	Balnc	1.7	12.3	14.1	–	–
Fidelity Growth America	USEq	– 0.7	19.3	20.3	20.9	–
Fidelity Int'l Portfolio	GloEq	1.8	21.6	18.6	15.9	12.7
Fidelity True North	CanEq	5.0	23.7	13.3	–	–
Scudder Canadian Equity	CanEq	3.6	16.1	17.8	–	–
Scudder Canadian Shrt Trm Bond	Mortg	1.7	2.7	4.8	–	–
Scudder Global	GloEq	5.6	19.7	17.7	–	–
Scudder Greater Europe	Europ	0.6	14.9	21.1	–	–
Scudder US Growth & Income	USEq	– 5.0	6.2	15.5	–	–
Templeton Canadian Stock	CanEq	6.0	15.1	9.9	9.7	6.4
Templeton Int'l Stock	GloEq	8.3	22.3	14.2	12.8	13.6
Trimark Select Balanced	Balnc	9.9	13.8	8.8	9.7	–
Trimark Select Cdn Growth	CanEq	16.7	19.6	8.5	8.5	–
Trimark Select Growth	GloEq	6.8	24.8	10.5	11.4	13.3

(Source: BellCharts Inc., as of September 30, 1999)

Because the Generations Funds were recently launched and do not have a measurable previous track record, the performance of the underlying **mutual funds** without the addition of insurance charges is used. Information on the TDQC (Toronto Dominion Quantitative Capital) funds were unavailable at the time of publishing.

Concordia Investment Funds

Descriptive Overview of the Insurance Company

Concordia Life Insurance Company
Ratings:
A– (Excellent) — A.M. Best & Company
Assets:
Over $ 3 billion as part of Empire Financial Group

Concordia Life Insurance Company is a member of Empire Financial Group, an organization with more than 75 years experience in Canada. Concordia itself currently has almost $1 billion in assets and offers a portfolio of investment and protection life and money products.

Investment Fund Manager
Empire Financial Group

Death Benefit
The beneficiary is guaranteed to receive the greater of either the market value of the policy upon notification of the annuitant's death or the net original deposit amount. Any back-end load charges will not apply.

Maturity Benefit

At the end of the policy term of at least 10 years, the policyholder will receive either the current total market value of the plan or the original net investment calculated at 100% of total net deposits made more than five years ago and 75% of net deposits made within the last five years. If the maturity amount is more than $5,000, the client has a choice between a lump-sum payment or a regular income flow. Policies can be held up to age 90 for non-registered accounts.

Guarantee Reset Option

No resets are available at this time.

Purchase Options and Costs/Automatic Contribution Plan

The initial deposit must be at least $500 or $250 per fund, or $50 if an automatic contribution plan is set up. Funds may be purchased up to age 80 for non-registered policies and up to the current age legislation for registered policies, on a no-load or back-end load option on a six-year declining basis starting at 6.00%. Switches are permitted up to two times per year, after which there is a $50 charge for each switch. The annual management fee for each fund ranges from 1.63% to 2.27%, including the insurance cost.

Liquidity/Free-Redemption Criteria/Systematic Withdrawal Plan

Partial withdrawals may be requested at any time and investment fund units are calculated at market value, subject to back-end load charges. For non-registered policies, clients may redeem up to 10.00% of back-end load units held every year without any redemption fees or load charges applied. All withdrawals will proportionately decrease the principal guarantee.

(Source: Concordia Investment Funds, 1999)

Investment Fund Performance						
Fund Name	Fund Type	YTD	1 Year	3 Year	5 Year	10 Year
Concordia Bond	CaBnd	− 2.0	0.0	4.8	6.9	−
Concordia Equity	CdnEq	3.9	18.6	13.1	11.6	−
Concordia Money Market	CdnMM	2.9	4.0	3.4	4.2	−
Concordia Special Growth	CdnSm	− 1.1	3.3	1.9	13.8	−
Concordia Strategic Balanced	CaBal	0.9	9.0	8.2	−	−

(Source: BellCharts Inc., as of September 30, 1999)

The Co-operators Investment Funds

Descriptive Overview of the Insurance Company

The Co-operators Life Insurance Company
Ratings:
8+ — TRAC Rating Services
Assets:
Over $1 billion

The Co-operators Life Insurance Company is located in Regina, Saskatchewan, and is a member of the Co-operators Group of Companies which has assets exceeding $3.7 billion. It has 31 member owners, comprised of co-operatives, credit unions, and other similar organizations, with a combined membership of 5 million Canadians.

Investment Fund Manager
The Co-operators Investment Counselling Limited (CICL)

Death Benefit
Prior to age 75, the guaranteed death benefit payable is either the current market value of the funds, or at minimum, the sum of 100% of deposits made prior to the closing decade (10-year period preceding the policy maturity date) and 80% of deposits made during the closing decade, reduced proportionately by any withdrawals.

At age 75 and beyond, the death benefit will be the greatest of the fund value on the valuation date immediately following notification of death, 75% of all deposits made, or 80% of the maturity benefit if the maturity date was the date of notification of death. Any back-end load charges will not be applicable.

Maturity Benefit

The policy maturity period is selected by the holder and must be a minimum of 10 years, up to age 85 for non-registered policies. Upon maturity date, the amount payable will be either the market value or the guaranteed minimum consisting of the sum of 100% of deposits made prior to the closing decade (10-year period pre-ceding maturity date) and 80% of deposits made during the closing decade, reduced proportionately by any withdrawals.

Guarantee Reset Option

The policyholder may request up to two resets per calendar year prior to the closing decade, and not beyond age 59 for registered policies and age 75 for non-registered policies. Each reset will advance the maturity date by 10 years.

Purchase Options and Costs/Automatic Contribution Plan

A minimum $250 lump sum is required for initial purchase, or $25 if an automatic contribution plan is established, up to age 75 for non-registered policies and age 59 for registered policies. All funds are offered on a back-end load option, declining over seven years from 5.00% to 0.00%. The annual management fee for each fund is approximately 2.25%.

Liquidity/Free-Redemption Criteria/Systematic Withdrawal Plan

Partial redemptions of a minimum $500 may be requested at any time. Fund units are calculated at market value and, for non-registered policies, clients may redeem up to 10.00% of the previous week's fund value once every calendar year. Second and subse-quent partial redemptions within the calendar year will be subject to a $25 service fee plus any applicable back-end load charges if beyond the 10.00% allowance. All withdrawals will proportionately decrease the guarantee benefits.

No systematic withdrawal plans are available at this time.

(Source: the Co-operators, 1999)

Investment Fund Performance						
Fund Name	Fund Type	YTD	1 Year	3 Year	5 Year	10 Year
Co-operators Balanced	CaAsA	– 2.6	4.2	7.4	9.9	–
Co-operators Cdn Equity	CdnLC	2.4	14.5	8.7	8.5	–
Co-operators Fixed Income	CaBnd	– 1.8	– 0.4	7.6	9.8	–
Co-operators Money Market	CdnMM	2.2	3.0	–	–	–
Co-operators US Diversified	GlBal	– 10.8	– 6.0	–	–	–
Co-operators US Equity	USEqt	– 13.6	2.8	7.0	18.5	–

(Source: BellCharts Inc., as of September 30, 1999)

CUMIS MemberFunds

Descriptive Overview of the Insurance Company

CUMIS Life Insurance Company
Ratings:
8+ — TRAC Rating Services
Assets:
$660 million

The CUMIS Life Insurance Company, a subsidiary of the CUMIS Group Limited, has served credit unions, *caisse populaires*, and financial co-operatives and their members since 1937. Incorporated in 1976, CUMIS, a joint stock insurance company centered in Burlington, Ontario, provides a diverse portfolio of insurance products and other non-financial services, ranging from life and accident/health policies and annuities to business development training programs and insurance technology support.

Investment Fund Manager
Guardian Capital Inc.

Death Benefit
Upon the death of the annuitant, the beneficiary is guaranteed to receive the greater of either the market value of the policy or the

net original deposit amount (which includes any withdrawals). Any back-end load charges will not apply.

Maturity Benefit

At the end of the policy term as designated by the client (minimum 10-year term and up to age 90), the guaranteed value of the policy is calculated based on total current market value or original net investment, whichever is higher. Clients may opt to reinvest the proceeds, receive installment payments, or purchase a life annuity.

Guarantee Reset Option

No resets are available at this time.

Purchase Options and Costs/Automatic Contribution Plan

The initial deposit must be a minimum of $500 per fund, or $50 per fund if a pre-authorized contribution plan is set up, up to age 90 for non-registered policies, and up to legislated age restrictions for RSP/RIF policies. All funds are purchased on a back-end load option based on a six-year schedule which declines from 6.00% in the first year.

Switches (or transfers) among funds, at a minimum $250 amount, are permitted up to four times per calendar year, after which there is a $50 administrative charge. The annual management fee for each fund ranges from 1.50% to 2.05%.

Liquidity/Free-Redemption Criteria/Systematic Withdrawal Plan

Partial withdrawals may be requested at any time, subject to a minimum amount of $500, and fund units are calculated based on current market value. An Automatic Withdrawal Plan (AWP) may be set up for payments of $100 or more on a regular basis provided that the policy value is at least $5,000.

Clients may redeem up to 10.00% of the value of their policies, as at December 31 of the previous calendar year, without any back-end load charges. This is a non-cumulative annual allowance. All withdrawals will proportionately decrease the guarantees.

(Source: CUMIS, 1999)

Investment Fund Performance						
Fund Name	Fund Type	YTD	1 Year	3 Year	5 Year	10 Year
CUMIS Life Canadian Balanced	CaBal	1.3	5.9	–	–	–
CUMIS Life Canadian Bond	CaBnd	– 1.4	– 0.3	–	–	–
CUMIS Life Canadian Growth Eq	CdnEq	5.1	15.1	–	–	–
CUMIS Life Global Balanced	GlBal	0.2	8.4	–	–	–
CUMIS Life Money Market	CdnMM	2.8	3.9	–	–	–

(Source: BellCharts Inc., as of September 30, 1999)

Empire Life Elite Investment Program

Descriptive Overview of the Insurance Company

Empire Life Insurance Company
Ratings:
A (Excellent) — A.M. Best & Company
8+ — TRAC Insurance Services Ltd.
Assets:
$3.7 billion

The Empire Life Insurance Company was incorporated on January 11, 1923, and recently celebrated 75 years as a leading provider of financial planning and insurance services. It has consistently demonstrated excellent capitalization and financial strength within the Canadian industry. Concordia Life Insurance Company is a wholly-owned subsidiary of Empire.

Investment Fund Manager
Empire Financial Group

Death Benefit
In the event of death, the beneficiary will receive the greater of either the current market value of the units or 100% of all deposits to age 65, plus 75% of all deposits made after age 65, less any proportionate withdrawals. Back-end load charges will be waived.

Maturity Benefit

The maturity period is selected by the client provided that it is at least 10 years from the date of issue. If no maturity date is selected, registered plans will mature at age 68 and non-registered plans will mature on the 10th anniversary date of the contract or the anniversary nearest age 85. The amount received will be the greater of either the market value or 75% of all net deposits.

Guarantee Reset Option

Policyholders may reset their guarantees up to two times per consecutive 12-month period, provided that their policy has at least 10 years remaining until the maturity date.

Purchase Options and Costs/Automatic Contribution Plan

Depending whether the Elite Investment Program or the Elite XL Investment Program is selected, the minimum initial purchase is $500 or $10,000 respectively, with additional deposit minimums of $500 or $1,000. Automatic monthly deposits of a minimum $30 or $100 (XL program) may be made monthly, quarterly, semi-annually, or annually. Subsequent deposits will increase the guarantee amount but do not affect the policy date or the maturity period.

Funds are available on a back-end load option, based on a five-year schedule, beginning at 5.00% and declining 1.00% per year, or on a no-charge basis for the XL program. The current annual management fee for each fund is approximately 2.40%.

Liquidity/Free-Redemption Criteria/Systematic Withdrawal Plan

With the Elite Investment Program, partial withdrawals may be requested by the client at any time and are subject to back-end load sales charges which are based on a five-year schedule beginning at 5.00% and declining 1.00% per year. The charge will be waived, however, on the first 1.00% of the total policy value if the automatic withdrawal is less than 2.00% of the policy value.

The Elite XL Investment Program allows up to four withdrawals per year without any applicable charges, after which a $50 service charge will apply.

Systematic partial withdrawals of a minimum $250 can be set up within all non-registered policies at a choice of frequency (monthly, quarterly, semi-annually, or annually). The guarantee amount will be proportionately reduced by each withdrawal. RRIF/LIF policies are permitted regular withdrawals based on legislated annual minimums without the stipulations mentioned.

(Source: Empire Life Insurance Company, 1999)

Investment Fund Performance						
Fund Name	Fund Type	YTD	1 Year	3 Year	5 Year	10 Year
Empire Asset Allocation	Balnc	1.5	10.7	7.8	8.5	–
Empire Balanced	Balnc	0.6	7.4	7.4	9.0	8.1
Empire Bond	Bond	– 1.9	– 0.6	5.6	7.6	8.3
Empire Dividend Growth	Divid	– 2.3	10.8	–	–	–
Empire Elite Equity 5	CanEq	4.4	19.1	10.0	10.9	7.7
Empire Equity Growth 3	CanEq	5.2	21.2	12.4	12.9	9.4
Empire Foreign Currency Cdn Bd	IntBd	– 1.0	– 0.2	4.0	3.2	–
Empire International	GloEq	– 1.4	14.7	12.5	11.2	11.7
Empire Money Market	CanMM	3.0	4.0	3.0	3.7	5.4
Empire Premier Equity 1	CanEq	5.1	20.6	11.6	12.0	8.7
Empire S & P 500 Index	USEq	2.3	23.5	–	–	–
Empire Small Cap Equity	SmCap	– 1.2	6.8	–	–	–

(Source: BellCharts Inc., as of September 30, 1999)

Great-West Life

Descriptive Overview of the Insurance Company

Great-West Life Assurance Company
Ratings:
AAA (c) — Duff & Phelps
AA+ — Standard & Poor's
A++ — A.M. Best & Company
Aa2 — Moody's Investor Services
Assets:
$6 billion (Cdn.)

The Great-West Life Assurance Company, based in Winnipeg, Manitoba, was incorporated on August 28, 1891, by a Special Act of the Parliament of Canada.

Investment Fund Managers
Great-West Life Investment Management Ltd.
Mackenzie Financial Corporation
AGF Funds Inc.
Sceptre Investment Counsel Limited
Beutel, Goodman & Company Ltd.
The Putnam Advisory Company, Inc.

Death Benefit

The death benefit will be the greater of either the total market value of the investment fund units at the next valuation date or 100% of all original deposits (less any withdrawals) into the investment funds. No age restrictions are stated, and back-end load charges will not be applicable. As of October 1999, clients will have to choose between a base product with a 75% death benefit or an enhanced product with a guarantee that increases to 100% after five years.

Maturity Benefit

The maturity date will be 10 years or more from the date of issue for registered contracts and at least 15 years for non-registered contracts. Upon maturity, the policyholder will receive the current market value of the contract, or the guarantee amount at either 75% or 100% of the original amount invested (less withdrawals) as selected by the client, toward the purchase of an annuity.

Guarantee Reset Option

The maturity benefit is reset every 10 years if the client chooses the enhanced product, with a 100% death and maturity benefit after five years.

Purchase Options and Costs/Automatic Contribution Plan

Two main plans are available: the Flexible Accumulation Annuity (FAA), registered or non-registered, and the Flexible Income Fund (FIF), essentially a retirement income fund account. Clients may purchase a non-registered contract up to age 90, and registered policies may be purchased up to age 69, in accordance with government age restrictions. The minimum lump-sum deposits may be as low as $300 for FAA policies or $50 if purchased through an automatic monthly plan. Guarantee periods are based on policy start date, and are not affected by any subsequent purchases.

The back-end load fee schedule starts at 4.50% on a seven-year declining basis. The annual management fee for "no load" funds ranges from 2.10% (bond funds) to 3.18% (equity funds). For "back-end load" funds, fees are about 0.25% lower.

Liquidity/Free-Redemption Criteria/Systematic Withdrawal Plan

Redemption or switches of any or all of the units held in a fund may be requested at any time prior to the maturity date or the death of the annuitant. The value of the units to be withdrawn will be based on the market value on the valuation date coinciding with or immediately following receipt of a client's withdrawal request. A systematic withdrawal plan can be set up at a monthly minimum amount of $50. Back-end fees are applicable and valuation of units is based on current market values of the next valuation date.

A partial withdrawal of up to 10.00% of back-end load units for registered and non-registered FAA policies and 20.00% for FIF policies can be made in any calendar year without any charges. This is a non-cumulative, annual allowance. The guarantee amount will decrease proportionate to each withdrawal.

(Source: Great-West Life, 1999)

Investment Fund Performance						
Fund Name	Fund Type	YTD	1 Year	3 Year	5 Year	10 Year
GWL Advanced Portfolio RS A	Balnc	3.6	13.2	8.1	–	–
GWL Advanced Portfolio RS B	Balnc	3.8	13.5	8.4	–	–
GWL Aggressive Portfolio RS A	Balnc	4.5	18.0	9.2	–	–
GWL Aggressive Portfolio RS B	Balnc	4.7	18.3	9.5	–	–
GWL American Growth A (AGF)	USEq	1.1	28.4	–	–	–
GWL American Growth B (AGF)	USEq	1.3	28.7	–	–	–
GWL Asian Growth A (AGF)	FarEa	17.1	47.8	–	–	–
GWL Asian Growth B (AGF)	FarEa	17.3	48.2	–	–	–
GWL Balanced (Beutel Goodman)A	Balnc	0.1	5.0	7.5	–	–
GWL Balanced (Beutel Goodman)B	Balnc	0.3	5.3	7.7	–	–
GWL Balanced (Mackenzie) A	Balnc	7.5	12.7	7.2	–	–
GWL Balanced (Mackenzie) B	Balnc	7.7	13.0	7.5	–	–
GWL Balanced (Sceptre) A	Balnc	– 0.9	5.1	7.1	–	–
GWL Balanced (Sceptre) B	Balnc	– 0.7	5.4	7.4	–	–
GWL Balanced Portfolio RS A	Balnc	3.3	12.7	8.9	–	–

Investment Fund Performance

Fund Name	Fund Type	YTD	1 Year	3 Year	5 Year	10 Year
GWL Balanced Portfolio RS B	Balnc	3.5	13.0	9.2	–	–
GWL Bond (Beutel Goodman) A	Bond	– 2.2	– 0.8	5.7	–	–
GWL Bond (Beutel Goodman) B	Bond	– 2.0	– 0.6	6.0	–	–
GWL Bond (Sceptre) A	Bond	– 2.4	– 1.5	6.4	–	–
GWL Bond (Sceptre) B	Bond	– 2.2	– 1.3	6.7	–	–
GWL Canadian Bond (G) A	Bond	– 1.6	– 0.2	5.9	7.7	8.1
GWL Canadian Bond (G) B	Bond	– 1.4	0.0	6.2	7.9	–
GWL Canadian Equity A	CanEq	11.0	31.7	6.6	7.5	7.7
GWL Canadian Equity B	CanEq	11.2	32.0	6.9	7.7	–
GWL Canadian Opportunity A (M)	CanEq	17.3	39.5	–	–	–
GWL Canadian Opportunity B (M)	CanEq	17.5	39.9	–	–	–
GWL Canadian Resources (AGF) A	Spec	22.6	14.2	– 12.3	–	–
GWL Canadian Resources (AGF) B	Spec	22.8	14.5	– 12.0	–	–
GWL Cdn Real Estate #1A (G)	Spec	4.8	6.3	8.5	5.4	0.6
GWL Cdn Real Estate #1B (G)	Spec	5.0	6.6	8.7	5.6	–
GWL Conservative Port RS A	Balnc	– 0.8	3.1	5.7	–	–
GWL Conservative Port RS B	Balnc	– 0.6	3.4	6.0	–	–
GWL Diversified RS A	Balnc	3.8	15.1	9.0	9.1	7.9
GWL Diversified RS B	Balnc	4.0	15.4	9.2	9.3	–
GWL Dividend A (G)	Divid	– 0.5	9.7	–	–	–
GWL Dividend B (G)	Divid	– 0.3	10.0	–	–	–
GWL Dividend/Growth A (M)	CanEq	– 0.8	8.5	–	–	–
GWL Dividend/Growth B (M)	CanEq	– 0.6	8.7	–	–	–
GWL Equity (Mackenzie) A	CanEq	– 0.6	8.3	8.6	–	–
GWL Equity (Mackenzie) B	CanEq	– 0.4	8.5	8.9	–	–
GWL Equity (Sceptre) A	CanEq	0.2	10.9	6.8	–	–
GWL Equity (Sceptre) B	CanEq	0.4	11.2	7.1	–	–
GWL Equity Index A	CanEq	6.6	22.8	8.6	9.1	6.1
GWL Equity Index B	CanEq	6.8	23.1	8.9	9.3	–
GWL Equity/Bond (G) A	Balnc	5.8	18.8	7.8	8.5	8.4
GWL Equity/Bond (G) B	Balnc	6.0	19.1	8.0	8.8	–
GWL European Equity A (Sceptre)	Europ	– 0.3	11.4	–	–	–
GWL European Equity B (Sceptre)	Europ	– 0.1	11.6	–	–	–
GWL Global Income (AGF) A	IntBd	– 9.3	– 8.4	4.6	–	–
GWL Global Income (AGF) B	IntBd	– 9.1	– 8.2	4.9	–	–
GWL Government Bond A	Bond	0.1	1.0	4.0	–	–

Investment Fund Performance

Fund Name	Fund Type	YTD	1 Year	3 Year	5 Year	10 Year
GWL Government Bond B	Bond	0.3	1.3	4.3	–	–
GWL Growth & Income (AGF) A	Balnc	3.5	13.8	0.9	–	–
GWL Growth & Income (AGF) B	Balnc	3.7	14.1	1.1	–	–
GWL Growth & Income (M) A	Balnc	– 1.5	3.5	8.4	–	–
GWL Growth & Income (M) B	Balnc	– 1.3	3.8	8.7	–	–
GWL Growth Equity (AGF) A	CanEq	9.3	15.9	2.8	–	–
GWL Growth Equity (AGF) B	CanEq	9.5	16.2	3.1	–	–
GWL Income (Mackenzie) A	Balnc	0.6	4.2	5.7	–	–
GWL Income (Mackenzie) B	Balnc	0.7	4.5	6.0	–	–
GWL Income A	Balnc	– 1.3	1.9	6.6	–	–
GWL Income B	Balnc	– 1.1	2.1	6.8	–	–
GWL Int'l Opportunity A (P)	GloEq	30.9	55.9	–	–	–
GWL Int'l Opportunity B (P)	GloEq	31.1	56.3	–	–	–
GWL International Bond A	IntBd	– 7.3	– 1.7	2.2	–	–
GWL International Bond B	IntBd	– 7.2	– 1.5	2.5	–	–
GWL International Equity A	GloEq	9.9	30.5	17.0	–	–
GWL International Equity B	GloEq	10.2	30.8	17.3	–	–
GWL Larger Company Equity (M) A	CanEq	3.1	12.6	5.3	–	–
GWL Larger Company Equity (M) B	CanEq	3.3	12.9	5.6	–	–
GWL Mid Cap Canada A (G)	SmCap	12.7	31.7	–	–	–
GWL Mid Cap Canada B (G)	SmCap	12.9	32.0	–	–	–
GWL Moderate Portfolio RS A	Balnc	0.7	7.4	6.8	–	–
GWL Moderate Portfolio RS B	Balnc	0.9	7.7	7.1	–	–
GWL Money Market A	CanMM	2.5	3.6	2.8	3.4	5.2
GWL Money Market B	CanMM	2.7	3.8	3.0	3.7	–
GWL Mortgage A	Mortg	– 1.0	0.1	5.2	6.9	7.7
GWL Mortgage B	Mortg	– 0.8	0.4	5.4	7.2	–
GWL North American Equity (BG) A	CanEq	4.9	11.9	10.2	–	–
GWL North American Equity (BG) B	CanEq	5.1	12.2	10.5	–	–
GWL Smaller Company Equity (M) A	SmCap	– 10.2	– 2.9	0.7	–	–
GWL Smaller Company Equity (M) B	SmCap	– 10.0	– 2.7	0.9	–	–
GWL US Equity A	USEq	– 2.2	18.2	20.4	–	–
GWL US Equity B	USEq	2.0	18.5	20.7	–	–

(Source: BellCharts Inc., as of September 30, 1999)

Hartford Life Investment Advantage Plus

Descriptive Overview of the Insurance Company

Hartford Life Insurance Company of Canada
Ratings:
n/a
Assets:
Over $200 billion (Hartford Financial Services Group)

The Hartford Life Insurance Company of Canada, originally incorporated as the Income Life Insurance Company of Canada in 1963, is a public stock life insurance company based in Burlington, Ontario, with over 30 years in operation. Hartford Life is owned by Hartford Life and Accident Insurance Company, a member company of the Hartford Financial Services Group, one of North America's oldest and largest international insurance and financial service operations.

Investment Fund Managers
Hartford Life
Hibernian Capital Management Ltd.
McLean Budden Ltd.
Porthmeor Securities Inc.
Yield Management Group Inc.

Death Benefit

Hartford Life guarantees that the beneficiary will receive the greatest of the market value of the policy at the next valuation date following the annuitant's death, 100% of total original deposits less withdrawals, or the highest policy value achieved on any policy anniversary date since issue, up to 200% of net deposits (to age 70). The guarantee is fixed at 100% for deposits made after age 70. Back-end load charges are applicable if the beneficiary entitlement is more than 100% of net deposits.

Maturity Benefit

Upon maturity, the owner will receive 100% of the net deposits, the current market value at the next valuation date, or the value as of the last reset, whichever is the highest. Valuation dates occur on the last business day of the week. The maturity period is selected by the client, provided it is at least 10 years.

Guarantee Reset Option

A maximum of two resets per calendar year is permitted for clients, through written request for the maturity and death benefit. A new maturity date of at least 10 more years will then be set. Resets are not accepted after age 70 for non-registered and RIF accounts or after age 69 for registered and locked-in contracts.

Purchase Options and Costs/Automatic Contribution Plan

Maximum age of issue for contracts is 79 years for non-registered accounts, 68 years for RRSPs, and 80 years for RRIFs.

The minimum initial deposit is $500 and/or $250 per fund by lump sum, and subsequent deposits must be at least $250 or $50 per fund. The minimum amount varies if an automatic contribution plan is set up. For automatic contributions, the minimum initial deposit is $250 and/or $50 per fund, and subsequent regular deposits must be at least $35 per fund. Subsequent deposits exceeding 50% of the accumulated value of the policy at the last anniversary date or exceeding $15,000 may be allowed only in a separate contract with a new maturity.

All funds are purchased on a back-end load basis of 6.00%, declining to 0.00% after six years. For each of the funds, the annual investment management fee ranges from 2.40% to 2.80%.

Liquidity/Free-Redemption Criteria/Systematic Withdrawal Plan

Up to two withdrawals per year can be requested by the client, after which an administration fee of $50 will be levied. An automatic withdrawal plan can be established for non-registered policies with an accumulated value of $5,000. RRIF/LIF policies are permitted regular withdrawals up to legislated annual minimums without the stipulations mentioned.

A maximum of 10.00% of the original value of all back-end load units purchased within the previous six years may be withdrawn in each calendar year without incurring charges. All types of withdrawals exceeding this allocation will be subject to applicable back-end load charges.

(Source: Hartford Life Insurance Company of Canada, 1999)

Investment Fund Performance						
Fund Name	Fund Type	YTD	1 Year	3 Year	5 Year	10 Year
Hartford Life Aggressive Growth	CdnSm	10.1	23.3	–	–	–
Hartford Life Asset Allocation	CaAsA	7.7	6.7	–	–	–
Hartford Life Cdn Advanced Tech	ScTec	– 13.4	11.9	–	–	–
Hartford Life Cdn Equity	CdnLC	1.4	18.2	–	–	–
Hartford Life Cdn Income	CaBnd	– 2.5	– 1.4	–	–	–
Hartford Life Money Market	CdnMM	1.8	2.6	–	–	–
Hartford Life Real Est Income	RlEst	9.9	18.7	–	–	–
Hartford Life Sel World Econs	GloEq	– 7.7	8.2	–	–	–

(Source: BellCharts Inc., as of September 30, 1999)

Imperial Life Millennia III

Descriptive Overview of the Insurance Company

Imperial Life Assurance Company of Canada
Ratings:
AA and AA (low) for DBRS — Standard & Poor's
Assets:
$5 Billion

This company was incorporated by an Act of the Parliament of Canada on April 23, 1896, to transact the business of life insurance and annuities. In 1994, Imperial Life became a subsidiary of Desjardins Laurentian Life Group.

Investment Fund Manager
Canagex Inc.

Death Benefit
The company guarantees that the death benefit will be the greater of either the current market value of the contract as calculated on receipt of written notification of the annuitant's death or 100% of the total deposits (less proportionate withdrawals) made before age 80. After age 80, the policy value is guaranteed at 80% if deposited within the last five years, 90% if within the last six or seven years, 95% if within the last eight or nine years, and 100% if deposited

more than 10 years prior to death. No back-end load charges are applicable.

Maturity Benefit

The initial maturity period must be a minimum of 10 years from the date of application. Upon maturity, the contract will be automatically renewed for a new term of 10 years, up to an age limit of 95 years. Alternatively, through written request, the policy may be surrendered for cash installment payments or a lump sum payment, valued at the greater of the guaranteed amount (100% of deposits less withdrawals) or current market value of the contract.

Guarantee Reset Option

Imperial Life allows a limit of twice per calendar year after the first six months for policy holders to reset their guarantee amounts, up to the age of 80 years. Each reset will be deemed to be a new deposit with a new 10-year maturity term.

Purchase Options and Costs/Automatic Contribution Plan

Initial deposits must be at least $500, however, this amount is not required if automatic deposits are set up for monthly contributions of at least $50. The total amount of deposits in the first 12 months must be at least $500. Subsequent deposits will not change the maturity date of the policy as stated at the time of application. Non-registered contracts must be established by age 90. Registered policies are subject to government age regulations.

At the time of purchase, two types of load options are available: back-end load based on a five-year declining fee schedule starting at 5.00%, or a no-load option with a higher management fee. The current annual management fee for each fund ranges from 1.53% to 2.45%; with the no-load option, the fee is 10 basis points higher per fund.

Liquidity/Free-Redemption Criteria/Systematic Withdrawal Plan

All partial withdrawals must be a minimum of $500, and if applicable, back-end load units will be charged a fee based on a declining schedule. The value of the contract must be at least $5,000 to set up a systematic withdrawal plan, and the withdrawal amount must be at least $25. Back-end load charges, if applicable, are waived under the withdrawal plan up to a non-cumulative maximum each year of 12.00% of the value of the contract. For registered plans (including RRIF/LIFs), back-end load charges can be waived under the same conditions without a systematic withdrawal plan. Every withdrawal will porportionately decrease the guarantee amount based on current market value.

(Source: Imperial Life Financial, 1999)

Investment Fund Performance						
Fund Name	Fund Type	YTD	1 Year	3 Year	5 Year	10 Year
Imperial Growth Canadian Eqty	CdnEq	− 0.2	11.6	4.9	6.4	6.3
Imperial Growth Diversified	CaBal	0.2	9.1	7.3	8.5	7.9
Imperial Growth Money Market	CdnMM	2.5	3.4	2.6	3.4	5.0
Imperial Growth N Amer Equity	USEqt	− 0.1	19.6	13.4	13.9	9.5

(Source: BellCharts Inc., as of September 30, 1999)

Industrial Alliance Ecoflex

Descriptive Overview of the Insurance Company

Industrial Alliance Life Insurance Company
Ratings:
n/a
Assets:
Over $7.5 billion, $2 billion in segregated funds

Since its inception in March 1969, the Industrial Alliance Life Insurance Company has offered a wide range of financial products and services to Canadians.

Investment Fund Managers
AGF Funds Inc.
Bissett & Associates Investment Management Ltd.
Fidelity Investments Canada Limited
Goodman & Company
National Life of Canada
State Street Global Advisors
Templeton Management Ltd.

Death Benefit
Upon the death of the annuitant, the beneficiary will receive the greater of either the current market value of the policy at the date

on which the company receives all documents required to settle the claim or 100% of the value of the original deposits (80% guarantee for subsequent deposits and deposits made after age 80).

Maturity Benefit

The maturity date for the policy must be selected between the 55th and the 69th birthdays of the client, and must be at least 10 years from the date of original investment. A change of maturity date may be requested in writing at any time. Any maturity date that has been deferred beyond the 80th birthday of the annuitant will be automatically renewed to the 100th birthday of the annuitant.

At maturity, the client will receive an amount equal to the market value or the Guaranteed Minimum Value (GMV). The GMV is established at 10 years before the maturity date or on December 31st of the year in which the annuitant reaches age 80, and will be calculated as the greater of either the market value on that date or the value of all original net deposits. All subsequent deposits made during the final 10 years of the contract or after age 80 are guaranteed at 80%. Clients may renew the contract, withdraw the investment, transfer to a registered plan, or purchase an annuity.

Guarantee Reset Option

Up to age 59, the client may request a change in the maturity date of the contract, at which time the GMV will be reset or increased to the current market value. The new maturity date must be at least 10 years after the date of request, and the request date must be in the age 55 to 69 period.

Purchase Options and Costs/Automatic Contribution Plan

Policyholders may invest their deposits among the available investment funds at a minimum of $25 per fund. The maximum age for non-registered policies is 90, and for registered policies up to the legislated age restriction (presently 69). Subsequent deposits and transfers between funds are permitted as long as the minimum amount per fund is maintained, and an automatic contribution system is available upon request. Each deposit received under the policy will have the same maturity date, but at a different guarantee level as outlined above.

Funds are available for purchase on a back-end load basis only, and the back-end load fee schedule begins at 5.00% and declines over seven years. The annual fund management fee currently ranges from 1.45% to 2.00% for each fund.

Liquidity/Free-Redemption Criteria/Systematic Withdrawal Plan

Partial withdrawals of at least $100 per fund from registered and/or non-registered policies may be requested at any time in writing by the client. Alternatively the client may join the Periodic Income Program (PIP), and elect to receive a regular income on a monthly (minimum $100) or annual (minimum $1000) basis, subject to a transaction fee.

RRIF/LIF policy holders are permitted regular withdrawals based on legislated annual minimums. The value of all investment fund units will be determined at current market value upon withdrawal, and a surrender charge may be applicable.

Surrender charges will not apply to redemptions of up to 10.00% of investment units within a policy during a calendar year. This right is not cumulative and cannot be carried forward to future years. The guarantee amount will decrease proportionate to all withdrawals.

(Source: Industrial Alliance Life Insurance Company, 1999)

Investment Fund Performance						
Fund Name	Fund Type	YTD	1 Year	3 Year	5 Year	10 Year
Industrial Alliance Eco A	CdnEq	3.9	15.4	4.3	6.9	–
Industrial Alliance Eco ABS	CdnEq	–	–	–	–	–
Industrial Alliance Eco AFI	CdnEq	–	–	–	–	–
Industrial Alliance Eco ANL	CdnLC	2.7	13.1	–	–	–
Industrial Alliance Eco B	CaBnd	– 0.9	0.3	5.3	7.5	–
Industrial Alliance Eco BBS	CaBnd	–	–	–	–	–
Industrial Alliance Eco BNL	CaBnd	– 1.7	– 0.1	–	–	–

Investment Fund Performance

Fund Name	Fund Type	YTD	1 Year	3 Year	5 Year	10 Year
Industrial Alliance Eco D	CaBal	4.1	11.8	6.8	8.2	–
Industrial Alliance Eco DNL	CaBal	1.0	7.9	–	–	–
Industrial Alliance Eco DO	CaBal	–	–	–	–	–
Industrial Alliance Eco DS	CaBal	–	–	–	–	–
Industrial Alliance Eco E	EmgEq	14.5	40.5	–	–	–
Industrial Alliance Eco G	FgnBd	– 9.8	– 9.3	–	–	–
Industrial Alliance Eco H	CaMtg	1.2	3.0	3.9	5.3	–
Industrial Alliance Eco I	USEqt	9.9	22.9	11.0	–	–
Industrial Alliance Eco KFI	EurEq	–	–	–	–	–
Industrial Alliance Eco M	CdnMM	2.5	3.5	2.9	3.6	–
Industrial Alliance Eco N	CdnEq	12.0	28.0	–	–	–
Industrial Alliance Eco NFI	CdnSm	–	–	–	–	–
Industrial Alliance Eco R	CdnSB	0.4	1.3	–	–	–
Industrial Alliance Eco S	USEqt	1.9	29.0	–	–	–
Industrial Alliance Eco T	CdnLC	10.6	23.1	–	–	–
Industrial Alliance Eco U	USEqt	– 2.2	18.9	–	–	–
Industrial Alliance Eco V	CaHIn	5.0	14.7	–	–	–

(Source: BellCharts Inc., as of September 30, 1999)

Infinity Segregated Funds

Descriptive Overview of the Insurance Company

Hartford Life Insurance Company of Canada
Ratings:
n/a
Assets:
Over $200 billion (Hartford Financial Services Group)

The Hartford Life Insurance Company of Canada, originally incorporated as the Income Life Insurance Company of Canada in 1963, is a public stock life insurance company based in Burlington, Ontario, with over 30 years in operation. Hartford Life is owned by Hartford Life and Accident Insurance Company, a member company of the Hartford Financial Services Group, one of North America's oldest and largest international insurance and financial service operations.

Investment Fund Manager
Infinity Investment Counsel Ltd.

Death Benefit
Upon notification of the annuitant's death, the beneficiary will receive the greatest of the current market value, 100% of the original net deposit, the value of the last reset, or the highest accu-

mulated value on any policy anniversary date up to two times (200%) the net amount deposited in the policy before age 71. All deposits made after age 71 are 100% guaranteed. Back-end load charges are not levied against death benefit proceeds.

Maturity Benefit
Upon maturity of a policy, which is a period of at least 10 years, the client, up to age 85, is entitled to receive the market value of the policy, the value of the last reset, or 100% of total deposits (less proportionate withdrawals), whichever is highest. This guarantee amount is reduced to 80% at the end of the calendar year in which the annuitant turns age 75.

Guarantee Reset Option
In any given year, the annuitant may reset the death and maturity guarantee amount up to two times, thus extending the contract a further 10 years.

Purchase Options and Costs/Automatic Contribution Plan
Policies may be issued up to age 84. The initial deposit for all policies is $500, with the exception of RRIF/LIF policies, which start at $10,000. Subsequent deposits must be at least $250 per policy, and $50 per fund. Monthly pre-authorized contributions can be made at a minimum of $35 per fund, with an initial deposit of $250 per policy and/or $50 per fund. Each deposit received under the policy will have a different guarantee date of 10 years.

Funds are available for purchase on a back-end load basis only, and the back-end load fee schedule begins at 5.50% and declines to 0.00% over seven years.

The annual management expense ratio currently ranges from 3.53% to 3.95% for each fund, which includes insurance costs of 0.73% to 1.00%.

Liquidity/Free-Redemption Criteria/Systematic Withdrawal Plan
Automatic withdrawal plans may be established in non-registered contracts, provided that the current policy value is more than

$5,000. All other partial withdrawals may be requested at any time provided that the remaining current policy value is not less than $500. An administrative fee of $50 will be charged after the first two withdrawals in a policy year. RRIF/LIF policy holders are permitted regular withdrawals based on legislated annual minimums without the stipulations mentioned and valued at current market prices.

An annual amount of up to 10.00% of back-end load fund holdings may be redeemed without surrender charges. The guarantee amount will decrease proportionate to all withdrawals.

(Source: Infinity Investment Counsel Ltd., 1999)

Investment Fund Performance						
Fund Name	Fund Type	YTD	1 Year	3 Year	5 Year	10 Year
Infinity Canadian	CdnEq	– 14.6	– 1.4	–	–	–
Infinity Income and Growth	Specl	– 0.5	3.2	–	–	–
Infinity International	USEqt	– 10.2	5.8	–	–	–
Infinity T-Bill	CdnMM	2.8	3.9	–	–	–
Infinity Wealth Management	Specl	– 16.3	3.1	–	–	–

(Source: BellCharts Inc., as of September 30, 1999)

Because the Infinity Segregated Funds were recently launched and do not have a measurable previous track record, the performance of the underlying **mutual funds** without the addition of insurance charges is used.

London Life Freedom Funds

Descriptive Overview of the Insurance Company

London Life Insurance Company
Ratings:
n/a
Assets:
Approximately $5 billion (segregated fund assets)

London Life, incorporated in 1874 in Ontario and in 1884 by an Act of the Parliament of Canada, is a subsidiary of the Great-West Life Assurance Company, and a member of the Power Financial Corporation group of companies.

Investment Fund Managers

AGF Funds Inc.
Beutel, Goodman & Company Ltd.
Fleming Canada Partners Inc.
GWL Investment Management Ltd.
London Life Investment Management Ltd.
Mackenzie Financial Corporation
Sceptre Investment Counsel Ltd.

Death Benefit

The beneficiary is guaranteed to receive the greater of either the current market value of the investment fund units within the policy or 100% of the total original deposit (less withdrawals). No age restrictions on deposits are listed, and back-end load charges do not apply.

Maturity Benefit
The maturity period is at least 10 years for both registered and non-registered accounts, and the maturity benefit is guaranteed to be no less than 75% of the total net amount deposited in a policy. Since several different options and plans are available, the length of the maturity period and the method of payment of the proceeds will vary according to each individual contract.

Guarantee Reset Option
No resets are available at this time.

Purchase Options and Costs/Automatic Contribution Plan
Investment funds can initially be purchased at a minimum of $300 (or $25 through an automatic contribution plan) for registered and non-registered plans and $10,000 for RIF accounts. All funds are on a back-end load basis only. Subsequent deposits must be at least $100 ($2,000 for RIF accounts) or $25 through an automatic plan. Since the policy is based on the contract date, the maturity date is not affected by any subsequent deposits. With the exception of government regulations on registered contracts, there are no age restrictions indicated.

The back-end load fee schedule starts at 5.00% and declines over seven years to 0.00%. The annual investment management fees range from 1.80% to 2.65% per fund.

Liquidity/Free-Redemption Criteria/Systematic Withdrawal Plan
Clients may request a total or partial withdrawal of a $500 minimum (or $1,000 for RIFs) at any time, provided that the total policy value remains at least $500 and/or $25 in each fund. Automatic withdrawals (from non-registered accounts) of a minimum $25 per month ($50 for RIFs) can be set up, provided that

the minimum requirements are met. The value of each withdrawal will be at market value, less any applicable back-end load charges, and will proportionately decrease the guarantee amount.

Non-registered and RIF contract holders are permitted annual withdrawals of up to 20.00%, on a scheduled basis only, without any applicable back-end load fees.

(Source: London Life, 1999)

Investment Fund Performance						
Fund Name	Fund Type	YTD	1 Year	3 Year	5 Year	10 Year
London Life Amer Eq (Maxxum)	USEqt	26.8	63.2	–	–	–
London Life Amer Growth (AGF)	USEqt	0.7	23.7	–	–	–
London Life Asian Growth (AGF)	AsPac	14.0	35.6	–	–	–
London Life Bal (B– G)	CaAsA	3.6	8.4	–	–	–
London Life Bal (Sceptre)	CaBal	– 0.3	5.8	–	–	–
London Life Bal Growth (LLIM)	CaBal	0.5	11.9	–	–	–
London Life Bond (LLIM)	CaBnd	– 1.7	– 0.2	5.4	8.0	7.8
London Life Cdn Bal (Maxxum)	CaBal	5.4	13.8	–	–	–
London Life Cdn Eq Gr (Maxxum)	CdnEq	5.3	23.5	–	–	–
London Life Cdn Equity (GWLIM)	CdnEq	12.2	31.1	–	–	–
London Life Cdn Equity (LLIM)	CdnLC	3.2	23.3	9.7	10.0	7.3
London Life Cdn Oppor (Mack)	ScTec	17.3	38.6	–	–	–
London Life Diversified (LLIM)	CaBal	0.5	11.4	9.3	9.8	8.5
London Life Dividend (LLIM)	CaDiv	0.3	13.4	–	–	–
London Life Dividend (Maxxum)	CaDiv	– 0.3	9.7	–	–	–
London Life Equity (Mack)	CdnEq	– 1.9	7.8	–	–	–
London Life Equity (Sceptre)	CdnEq	1.3	12.3	–	–	–
London Life Equity/Bond(GWLIM)	CaBal	7.0	18.0	–	–	–
London Life Euro Eq (Sceptre)	EurEq	0.3	12.7	–	–	–
London Life Global Eq (LLIM)	GloEq	3.4	23.6	–	–	–
London Life Global Eq (Maxxum)	GloEq	7.8	29.1	–	–	–
London Life Gov Bond (GWLIM)	CaBnd	0.1	0.9	–	–	–
London Life Growth & Inc (AGF)	CaAsA	1.7	11.2	–	–	–
London Life Growth & Inc(Mack)	CaAsA	– 2.2	3.2	–	–	–
London Life Growth Eq (AGF)	CdnEq	7.0	13.2	–	–	–
London Life Growth Eq (LLIM)	CdnEq	4.2	23.6	–	–	–
London Life Income (LLIM)	CaBnd	– 1.3	3.7	–	–	–

Investment Fund Performance

Fund Name	Fund Type	YTD	1 Year	3 Year	5 Year	10 Year
London Life Income (Mack)	CaBnd	0.7	4.0	–	–	–
London Life Income (Maxxum)	CaBnd	– 4.7	– 2.8	–	–	–
London Life Int'l Eq (Fleming)	IntEq	13.3	34.1	10.8	–	–
London Life Larger Comp (Mack)	CdnLC	3.3	13.2	–	–	–
London Life Mid Cap Can(GWLIM)	CdnSm	13.0	30.9	–	–	–
London Life Money Mkt (LLIM)	CdnMM	2.7	3.9	3.1	4.1	6.1
London Life Mortgage (LLIM)	CaMtg	0.2	2.1	4.9	6.5	7.7
London Life N Am Balncd (LLIM)	CaBal	– 1.5	8.0	–	–	–
London Life N Am Equity (B-G)	CdnEq	9.4	14.7	–	–	–
London Life Nat Res (Maxxum)	NatRs	17.3	17.4	–	–	–
London Life Prec Met (Maxxum)	PrMtl	13.4	5.5	–	–	–
London Life Real Estate(GWLIM)	RlEst	5.2	9.3	–	–	–
London Life US Equity (LLIM)	USEqt	– 4.9	13.5	22.3	18.7	10.9

(Source: BellCharts Inc., as of September 30, 1999)

Mackenzie Segregated Funds

Descriptive Overview of the Insurance Company

Great-West Life Assurance Company
Ratings:
AAA (c) — Duff & Phelps
AA+ — Standard & Poor's
A++ — A.M. Best & Company
Aa2 — Moody's Investor Services
Assets:
$6 billion (Cdn.)

The Great-West Life Assurance Company, based in Winnipeg, Manitoba, was incorporated on August 28, 1891, by a Special Act of the Parliament of Canada, and is one of the largest providers of segregated funds in the country today.

Investment Fund Manager
Mackenzie Investment Management Inc.

Death Benefit
Upon notification of the client's death, the beneficiary will be paid an amount that is the greater of either the current market value or 75% of the original investment, less any withdrawals. Any back-end load charges will be waived. An Enhanced Guarantee rider will be

available in late 1999 at an additional cost that includes a reset of the guarantee amount every 10 years prior to the client's 70th birthday, and an increase of the guarantee percentage up to 100%, if the deposits are five years or more in duration.

Maturity Benefit

The owner will receive, upon maturity, the greater of either the current market value of the policy or 75% of the total original deposits, less proportionate withdrawals. Policies may be held up to a maximum age of 100 for non-registered accounts. An Enhanced Guarantee rider will also be available as described above.

Guarantee Reset Option

Two types of resets are currently available:

The Age 69 Reset feature entitles the client to a reset of the basic guarantee amount at current market value if the contract was issued on or before December 31 of the year in which the annuitant turned 59. A payment will be made to the contract if the current market value is less than 75% of the original investment on the last valuation day coinciding with or immediately preceding December 31 in the year in which the annuitant turns 69. This payment will be made in the form of money market investment units.

Clients may also select the Enhanced Guarantee rider, which provides for a reset of the guarantee amount every 10 years on the renewal date, prior to age 70, and, if the market value is lower than the guarantee amount of a contract, a Top-Up Benefit will add the difference to the contract in the form of money market investment units.

Purchase Options and Costs/Automatic Contribution Plan

A contract may be purchased up to age 90 if non-registered, and subject to current government age restrictions for registered policies. Subsequent deposits, in lump-sum or through an automatic plan, will each carry a separate maturity period of 10 years.

Funds may be purchased on a front-end load of 2.00%, or on a back-end load option based on a seven-year declining schedule that starts between 3.30% and 5.50%, depending on the fund selected. The current management expense ratio ranges from 1.83% to 2.55% per fund, and for the Enhanced Guarantee, there is an additional cost of 0.10% to 0.15%.

Liquidity/Free-Redemption Criteria/Systematic Withdrawal Plan

Partial withdrawals and transfers may be requested at any time, subject to any back-end load charges if applicable. All investment units will be valued at current market prices. A regular withdrawal program can be set up on a regular basis (i.e. monthly, semi-monthly, quarterly, etc.) at a specified amount if the value of the contract is at least $5,000.

Clients may withdraw up to 10.00% of back-end load fund units purchased in the contract during the current calendar year, plus 10.00% of the contract value as of December 31st of the previous calendar year, without incurring any charges.

(Source: Mackenzie Financial, 1999)

Investment Fund Performance						
Fund Name	Fund Type	YTD	1 Year	3 Year	5 Year	10 Year
Cundill Canadian Balanced C	CaBal	15.2	–	–	–	–
Cundill Canadian Security A	CdnSm	25.0	28.1	18.8	16.8	10.0
Cundill Value A	GloEq	27.0	30.3	6.2	8.4	9.0
Industrial American	USEqt	0.6	17.8	15.1	13.5	10.7
Industrial Balanced	CaBal	9.8	15.9	9.1	9.0	–
Industrial Bond	CaBnd	– 1.0	0.5	7.5	9.6	9.0
Industrial Cash Management	CdnMM	3.2	4.3	3.6	4.4	6.1
Industrial Dividend Growth	CaDiv	– 1.2	9.5	12.1	11.5	7.7
Industrial Growth	CdnEq	20.6	11.3	2.0	2.9	3.8
Industrial Horizon	CdnLC	3.3	12.6	8.6	7.3	6.4
Industrial Income A	CaBal	1.5	6.0	6.8	8.7	7.9
Industrial Pension	CaBal	– 1.3	5.6	10.8	10.6	6.3
Industrial Short-Term	CdnMM	2.5	3.4	2.7	3.6	–
Ivy Canadian	CdnEq	– 3.2	7.4	10.0	11.9	–
Ivy Enterprise	CdnSm	– 10.0	– 1.8	3.0	7.1	–
Ivy Foreign Equity	GloEq	3.0	19.7	17.8	16.2	–

Investment Fund Performance

Fund Name	Fund Type	YTD	1 Year	3 Year	5 Year	10 Year
Ivy Growth and Income	CaBal	– 2.6	3.3	9.8	12.6	–
Ivy Mortgage	CaMtg	0.7	2.7	4.2	6.2	–
STAR Cdn Balanced Growth & Inc	CaBal	– 3.0	4.3	7.8	–	–
STAR Cdn Conserv Inc & Growth	CaBal	– 2.2	1.9	–	–	–
STAR Cdn Long-Term Growth	CaBal	– 3.7	4.4	–	–	–
STAR Cdn Max Equity Growth	CdnEq	1.4	13.1	9.5	–	–
STAR Cdn Max Long-Term Growth	CaBal	0.2	10.6	–	–	–
STAR Invstmt Bal Growth & Inc	GlBal	– 1.8	5.2	8.2	–	–
STAR Invstmt Conserv Inc & Gr	GlBal	– 1.0	4.9	7.2	–	–
STAR Invstmt Long-Term Growth	GlBal	– 2.4	5.5	7.8	–	–
STAR Invstmt Max Long-Trm Grth	GlBal	– 1.4	10.0	5.2	–	–
Universal Americas	GloEq	2.1	17.7	7.6	5.2	8.0
Universal Canadian Balanced	CaBal	– 7.1	1.4	–	–	–
Universal Canadian Growth	CdnEq	– 3.2	5.4	10.5	–	–
Universal European Opportunits	EurEq	11.2	21.7	22.3	24.4	–
Universal Future	CdnEq	18.7	41.8	16.2	14.5	10.2
Universal Select Managers	GloEq	21.5	64.9	–	–	–
Universal World Balanced RRSP	GlBal	– 1.2	13.6	11.0	10.8	–
Universal World Growth RRSP	GloEq	1.9	21.9	10.1	10.1	–
Universal World Income RRSP	FgnBd	– 7.9	– 6.6	5.5	7.3	–
Universal World Tactical Bond	FgnBd	– 9.5	– 8.5	6.8	–	–
Universal World Value	GloEq	6.7	25.8	–	–	–

(Source: BellCharts Inc., as of September 30, 1999)

Because the Mackenzie Segregated Funds were recently launched and do not have a measurable previous track record, the performance of the underlying **mutual funds** without the addition of insurance charges is used.

Manulife Guaranteed Investment Funds (GIF Encore)

Descriptive Overview of the Insurance Company

Manufacturers Life Insurance Company
Ratings:
n/a
Assets:
Over $46 billion

Manulife Financial is a leading international financial services company, offering a variety of insurance, investment, and retirement products to individuals, families, and businesses.

Investment Fund Managers
AGF Group of Funds
AIM GT Global Canada Inc.
C.I. Capital Management
Elliott & Page Limited
Fidelity Investments
Goodman & Company, Investment Counsel
O'Donnell Investment Management Corporation
Talvest Fund Management Inc.
Trimark Investment Management Inc.

Death Benefit

With the automatic reset feature as explained below, the basic death benefit is guaranteed to be at least 100% of original deposits, and increased by at least a 4% interest rate, up to age 80. This applies for all accounts except LIF/RIF/LRIF policies. The beneficiary will receive the full death benefit guarantee amount, which is the greatest of the current market value, the total original deposit (less proportionate withdrawals) increased at an annual 4% interest rate up to age 80, or the value as of the last reset when the policy is renewed. Any back-end load charges will be waived.

Maturity Benefit

The owner will receive, upon maturity, an amount that is the greater of either the current market value of the policy or 100% of total deposits, less proportionate withdrawals. When a contract is renewed for a further 10-year term, the higher of either the value of the maturing deposit or the current market value will constitute the new deposit value. Policies may be held up to age 100 for non-registered accounts, with the guarantee at 80% during the final decade.

Guarantee Reset Option

The death benefit is automatically reset every year at 4% interest or at the current market value of the policy on each anniversary date, whichever yields the higher rate of return. This feature is not available for LIF/RRIF/LRIF policies. There are no resets for the maturity guarantee except at each 10-year anniversary date when the policy is renewed. The automatic reset does not affect the contract maturity date.

Purchase Options and Costs/Automatic Contribution Plan

To establish a contract, the maximum age of the annuitant is 90 for non-registered policies, 80 for LIFs, and 69 for LIRAs and RSPs. The minimum amount is $2,500 or $500 per fund, and for index fund contracts, the minimum is $500. If an automatic contribution plan is chosen, the minimum is $100 monthly. Subsequent deposits will each mature at 10 years from the next anniversary date.

Funds may be purchased on a front-end basis of 1.00% to 3.00%, or on a back-end load option based on a seven-year declining schedule that starts at 5.50% for balanced and equity funds and 4.50% for bond and dividend funds. The current annual management fee ranges from 1.90% to 2.80% per fund, with a management expense ratio ranging from 2.15% to 3.37%.

Liquidity/Free-Redemption Criteria/Systematic Withdrawal Plan
Partial withdrawals are permitted at any time, subject to any back-end load charges, as long as the value of the contract remains above $2,500 or $500 per fund. Scheduled withdrawals can also be set up monthly, quarterly, semi-annually, or annually.

A maximum of 10.00% of back-end load fund units purchased during a calendar year plus 10% of fund holdings at the end of the previous calendar year may be redeemed without incurring any fees. For RRIF/LIF contracts, the same provision applies at 20.00%.

An early withdrawal fee of 2.00% is levied if a withdrawal is made within 90 days of the policy start date. This is not applicable to RRIF/LIF/LRIF contracts or to systematic withdrawal plans.

(Source: Manulife Financial, 1999)

Investment Fund Performance						
Fund Name	Fund Type	YTD	1 Year	3 Year	5 Year	10 Year
AGF America Growth Class	USEqt	1.7	29.8	30.3	27.9	17.5
AGF Canadian Bond	CaBnd	− 1.8	− 0.6	6.8	9.2	9.3
AGF Canadian Growth & Income	CaAsA	4.1	15.1	3.0	8.7	7.7
AGF Canadian High Income	CaBal	− 0.6	1.0	5.2	7.3	7.8
AGF Canadian Stock	CdnEq	6.7	23.7	10.3	9.2	7.6
AGF Dividend	CaDiv	− 1.2	8.7	13.5	14.2	10.7
AGF Global Government Bond	FgnBd	− 8.6	− 7.7	6.0	7.4	8.8
AIM America Growth Class	USSml	4.3	35.0	11.0	−	−
AIM Canada Growth Class	CdnEq	4.5	27.6	6.7	−	−
Atlas Canadian Balanced	CaBal	− 1.1	7.4	11.4	12.3	8.9
Atlas Canadian Large Cap Growth	CdnLC	− 4.7	8.4	9.7	11.7	6.9
BPI Global Equity Value	GloEq	7.0	29.0	22.0	16.7	13.4
C.I. Global	GloEq	1.4	19.8	17.4	12.3	12.3
C.I. Harbour	CdnEq	8.3	19.4	−	−	−

Investment Fund Performance

Fund Name	Fund Type	YTD	1 Year	3 Year	5 Year	10 Year
C.I. Harbour Growth & Income	CaBal	0.4	7.4	–	–	–
Dynamic Dividend Growth	CaDiv	3.6	6.7	8.7	11.2	8.5
Dynamic Global Bond	FgnBd	– 9.6	– 7.6	– 2.3	3.6	6.3
Dynamic Partners	CaAsA	1.9	5.6	5.9	6.9	10.2
Elliott & Page American Growth	USEqt	1.5	24.5	24.8	20.7	14.3
Elliott & Page Balanced	CaBal	– 1.5	7.3	4.6	7.3	8.7
Elliott & Page Equity	CdnLC	11.6	25.3	4.2	8.1	8.6
Elliott & Page Money	CdnMM	3.0	4.2	3.6	4.4	6.3
Elliott & Page Sector Rotation	CdnLC	16.4	–	–	–	–
Elliott & Page Value Equity	CdnLC	5.9	22.1	–	–	–
Fidelity Capital Builder	CdnLC	1.6	15.0	– 0.2	3.7	5.6
Fidelity Cdn Asset Allocation	CaAsA	1.7	12.3	14.1	–	–
Fidelity Cdn Bond	CaBnd	– 1.1	0.3	6.5	7.6	7.8
Fidelity European Growth	EurEq	– 8.0	7.4	18.2	17.3	–
Fidelity Growth America	USEqt	– 0.7	19.3	20.3	20.9	–
Fidelity Int'l Portfolio	GloEq	1.8	21.6	18.6	15.9	12.7
Fidelity True North	CdnEq	5.0	23.7	–	–	–
MLI Aggressive Ass All GIF enc	CdnEq	1.7	–	–	–	–
MLI Balanced Asset All GIF enc	CaBal	0.7	–	–	–	–
MLI Cdn Equity Index GIF	CdnEq	7.3	24.0	–	–	–
MLI Conserv Ass All GIF enc	CaBnd	0.1	–	–	–	–
MLI Growth Asset Alloc GIF enc	CdnEq	0.4	–	–	–	–
MLI Moderate Asset All GIF enc	CaBal	– 0.6	–	–	–	–
MLI US Equity Index GIF	USEqt	– 0.4	21.2	–	–	–
Merrill Lynch Global Growth	GloEq	– 2.8	–	–	–	–
Merrill Lynch US Basic Value	USEqt	1.2	–	–	–	–
O'Donnell Cdn	CdnLC	4.5	17.9	–	–	–
O'Donnell Select	CdnEq	7.6	15.2	–	–	–
Sceptre Balanced Growth	CaBal	– 2.8	2.0	6.2	10.6	9.3
Sceptre Canadian Equity	CdnEq	1.8	12.4	–	–	–
Talvest Cdn Asset Allocation	CaAsA	5.1	16.0	11.9	11.3	8.9
Talvest Income	CdnSB	1.0	2.0	4.3	6.5	7.7
Talvest Value Line US Eq	USEqt	1.1	27.0	18.3	21.5	–
Trimark Select Balanced	CaBal	9.9	13.8	8.8	9.7	–
Trimark Select Cdn Growth	CdnEq	16.7	19.6	8.5	8.5	–
Trimark Select Growth	GloEq	6.8	24.8	10.5	11.4	13.3

(Source: BellCharts Inc., as of September 30, 1999)

Maritime Life Segregated Funds

Descriptive Overview of the Insurance Company

Maritime Life Assurance Company
Ratings:
A+ (Superior) — A.M. Best & Company
A1 — Moody's Investor Services
Assets:
$6.0 billion

Maritime Life was founded in Halifax, Nova Scotia, and incorporated in 1922. The company is organized into three product lines: group insurance, individual life, and investment products. In 1969, it was purchased by the John Hancock Mutual Life Insurance Company of Boston, one of the largest and most highly respected financial services companies in the United States, with a rating of A++ by A.M. Best & Company. It currently has approximately $100 billion U.S. under administration.

Investment Fund Managers
John Hancock Life Insurance Company
Altamira Investment Services
J.R. Senecal & Associates
TAL Investment Counsel

Death Benefit

The beneficiary will receive the greatest of the current market value of the contract, 100% of net deposits made before the end of the year in which the annuitant is age 76, or the policy value as of the last reset. The guarantee percentage will decline by 5% per year for deposits made after age 76 to a guarantee amount of 80% at age 80 and beyond. Back-end load charges are not applicable.

Maturity Benefit

Maritime Life's Stock Market Guarantee, through automatic daily resets, protects the highest value achieved by the plan in the years prior to the final 10-year term to maturity; subsequent deposits made in the final 10 years are guaranteed by 75%. The maturity date for the entire policy is chosen by the client, provided it is at least 10 years and not beyond age 90. Upon expiration of the policy, the client will receive either the market value or the guarantee amount, whichever is higher.

Guarantee Reset Option

Automatic daily resets in the years prior to the final 10-year term of a policy will lock in the death and maturity guarantee at the highest value achieved by the plan.

Purchase Options and Costs/Automatic Contribution Plan

Maritime Life currently offers three different Investment Plans: the Maritime Life Investment Account, the Investment Portfolio, and the Capital Accumulator. The maximum issue age for all non-registered accounts is age 80 and, for registered accounts, age 68 for the Investment Account RSP, age 90 for the Investment Account RIF, and age 59 for the Capital Accumulator RSP.

The Investment Portfolio and Investment Account may be set-up at a minimum initial deposit of $1,000 for RRSP accounts, $25,000 for RRIFs, and $5,000 for non-registered accounts. Clients may choose an automatic deposit plan on a periodic basis at an amount greater than or equal to $100. Each subsequent deposit (at least $100 for registered accounts and $500 for non-registered) will carry a separate maturity date based on the contract period that the client has selected. During the period before the final 10-year term, when an automatic reset occurs (i.e. if the market value of the contract reaches a new higher market value), a new maturity date will be established for the entire contract, which means that all deposits made up to that point will no longer have separate maturity dates. However, deposits made during the final 10 years of a policy will continue to have separate maturity dates because no resets are allowed during that time period.

All fund purchases are available on a back-end load basis at a seven-year declining schedule starting at 6.00%, or alternatively, for the Investment Portfolio only, an initial sales charge (ISC) option of 0.00% to 5.00% may be selected.

The Capital Accumulator account may be established at a minimum amount of $500, or a pre-authorized contribution plan of $30 per month. Clients will receive a bonus on the 15th policy anniversary and on every fifth policy anniversary thereafter. The bonus will be equal to 10% of the sum of all deposits made 10 or more years prior to the bonus date less any withdrawals.

There is an administration fee of $50 per year if total deposits are less than $5,000 (or monthly deposits are less than $50 each), $25 per year if total deposits are greater than or equal to $5,000 but less than $10,000, and no fee for deposits greater than or equal to $10,000 (or minimum $100 monthly deposits). Transfers between investment funds are permitted, however, a $25 charge per transfer may be levied if more than five are made in a year.

Investment funds are available on a back-end load basis that starts at 10.00% in the first year and declines to 0.00% after the 10th year.

The management expense ratios for all investment funds range from 1.80% for the Bond fund to 2.75% for Global funds.

Liquidity/Free-Redemption Criteria/Systematic Withdrawal Plan

Clients may request partial withdrawals of minimum $1,000 at any time, subject to any applicable back-end load charges and a transaction fee of $25 per withdrawal (except the Investment Portfolio account). Each withdrawal will proportionately decrease the guarantee amount.

Investment Portfolio and Investment Account clients may establish a systematic withdrawal plan at a minimum amount of $100 monthly, provided that the total accumulated value is at least $25,000. They may also withdraw, without any charges, up to 10.00% of the value of back-end load units held in the contract as of December 31, plus 10.00% of net deposits made throughout the year. RRIF/LIF policy holders are permitted regular withdrawals up to the legislated annual minimum without charges, and the units will be valued at current market prices.

(Source: Maritime Life, 1999)

Investment Fund Performance						
Fund Name	Fund Type	YTD	1 Year	3 Year	5 Year	10 Year
Maritime Life Aggressive EqA&C	CdnEq	11.7	32.8	–	–	–
Maritime Life Am Gr & Inc A&C	USEqt	– 6.8	8.8	16.3	17.2	–
Maritime Life Balanced A & C	CaBal	1.9	10.1	8.3	9.7	8.0
Maritime Life Bond A	CaBnd	– 0.5	0.8	5.6	7.6	8.2
Maritime Life Cdn Equity A & C	CdnLC	4.8	25.4	7.8	–	–
Maritime Life Discovery A & C	USSml	8.6	46.0	–	–	–
Maritime Life Dividend Inc A	CaDiv	– 3.2	7.4	9.5	–	–
Maritime Life Divrsfd Eqty A&C	CdnEq	2.7	20.2	–	–	–
Maritime Life EurAsia A & C	IntEq	10.1	27.3	–	–	–
Maritime Life Europe A & C	EurEq	2.3	20.4	–	–	–
Maritime Life Global Eq A&C	GloEq	– 4.0	16.9	12.5	–	–
Maritime Life Growth A & C	CdnEq	5.2	19.2	8.3	9.6	6.4
Maritime Life Money Market A	CdnMM	2.9	3.9	3.0	3.5	5.3
Maritime Life Pacif Basin EqAC	AsPac	23.5	52.4	– 4.0	– 2.9	
Maritime Life S&P 500 A & C	USEqt	2.7	24.3	20.4	–	–

(Source: BellCharts Inc., as of September 30, 1999)

National Life Ultraflex

Descriptive Overview of the Insurance Company

National Life Assurance Company of Canada
Ratings:
A (Excellent) — A.M. Best & Company
A — TRAC Insurance Services Ltd.
Passed all eight early warning solvency tests administered by TRAC Insurance Services Ltd.
Assets:
$7.6 billion — Industrial-Alliance consolidated assets

Founded in 1899, National Life is a member of the Industrial-Alliance Group of Companies. It currently ranks as one of the largest life and health insurance companies owned and operated in Canada.

Investment Fund Manager
National Life (Retirement and Investment Products Division)

Death Benefit
The beneficiary will receive the greatest of the current market value, the policy value as of the last reset, or 100% of deposits made to age 65 and 90% of deposits made after age 65, less any proportionate withdrawals and applicable back-end load fees.

Maturity Benefit

The client may choose any maturity date that is at least 10 years from the issue date. Deposits held for more than five years in the policy are 100% guaranteed; the guarantee is 75% for deposits held less than five years. At maturity, the client will receive the guarantee amount, the current market value, or the policy value as of the last reset, whichever is highest, less proportionate withdrawals.

Guarantee Reset Option

Guarantees may be reset up to two times per calendar year through written request signed by the client. At age 65, the death guarantee cannot be reset and no further resets, for either the death or maturity guarantee, are allowed after age 85. Each reset will extend the maturity period a further 10 years.

Purchase Options and Costs/Automatic Contribution Plan

The minimum purchase amount is $500. A pre-authorized contribution plan is available on a minimum $50 monthly basis. Each subsequent deposit will not affect the contract maturity date, but the guarantee amount will vary according to the length of time the deposit is held within the policy, as outlined in the maturity benefit.

Funds may be purchased on a no-load or back-end load basis. The fee schedule for back-end funds begins at 5.00% and declines to 0.00% over six years, and the annual management fees range from 1.60% to 2.40% per fund.

Liquidity/Free-Redemption Criteria/Systematic Withdrawal Plan

Scheduled withdrawal plans are currently available at a minimum amount of $50 monthly. Clients may withdraw up to 10.00% of the accumulated value of the policy each year, without back-end load charges, based on the anniversary date. Partial withdrawals that exceed this allocation, including those from RRIF/LIF policies, will be subject to back-end load charges, and will proportionately decrease the guarantee amount.

(Source: National Life, 1999)

Investment Fund Performance

Fund Name	Fund Type	YTD	1 Year	3 Year	5 Year	10 Year
Maritime Life Aggressive EqA&C	CdnEq	11.7	32.8	–	–	–
Maritime Life Am Gr & Inc A&C	USEqt	– 6.8	8.8	16.3	17.2	–
Maritime Life Balanced A & C	CaBal	1.9	10.1	8.3	9.7	8.0
Maritime Life Bond A	CaBnd	– 0.5	0.8	5.6	7.6	8.2
Maritime Life Cdn Equity A & C	CdnLC	4.8	25.4	7.8	–	–
Maritime Life Discovery A & C	USSml	8.6	46.0	–	–	–
Maritime Life Dividend Inc A	CaDiv	– 3.2	7.4	9.5	–	–
Maritime Life Divrsfd Eqty A&C	CdnEq	2.7	20.2	–	–	–
Maritime Life EurAsia A & C	IntEq	10.1	27.3	–	–	–
Maritime Life Europe A & C	EurEq	2.3	20.4	–	–	–
Maritime Life Global Eq A&C	GloEq	– 4.0	16.9	12.5	–	–
Maritime Life Growth A & C	CdnEq	5.2	19.2	8.3	9.6	6.4
Maritime Life Money Market A	CdnMM	2.9	3.9	3.0	3.5	5.3
Maritime Life Pacif Basin EqAC	AsPac	23.5	52.4	– 4.0	– 2.9	
Maritime Life S&P 500 A & C	USEqt	2.7	24.3	20.4	–	–

(Source: BellCharts Inc., as of September 30, 1999)

NN Financial IMS III

Descriptive Overview of the Insurance Company

NN Financial (member of the ING Group)
Ratings:
A- (Excellent) — A.M. Best & Company
Assets:
Over $1 billion, shared assets with ING Group of $360 billion

NN Financial was established in 1989 through the merger of Halifax Life and MONY Life of Canada. The company has earned an enviable reputation as an industry leader through its more than 100-year history. It derives benefits from membership in the ING Group, an international financial organization based in the Netherlands, which operates network banking and insurance businesses in 58 countries.

Investment Fund Managers
ING Investment Management Inc.
Jones Heward Investment Counsel
Newcastle Capital Management Inc.
RT Capital Management Inc.

Death Benefit
The client can select a guarantee of 75% or 100% of net deposits

(including withdrawals) for both non-registered and registered accounts. For non-registered policies, if the client is over the age of 81, the 100% guarantee drops to 80%. The beneficiary will receive an amount equal to the greatest of the guarantee selected by the client, the current market value of the contract on the date of notification of the annuitant's death, or the policy value as of the last reset, less any outstanding back-end load charges.

Maturity Benefit

Policy maturity periods must be at least 10 years and can only be held up to age 69 (on the birthday of the client) for registered policies, and age 100 for non-registered policies. As in the death benefit, clients may select a 75% or a 100% guarantee. Any deposits made in the last decade of a 100% guarantee policy, however, have a reduced guarantee of 80%. Clients may switch between guarantee options during the life of the policy, but the maturity date will be extended in cases where the guarantee is increased.

At maturity, the policy will be automatically renewed unless NN Financial is otherwise instructed by the client. The client will be entitled to an amount equal to the guarantee selected, the current market value of the contract on maturity date, or the value as of the last reset, whichever is highest.

Guarantee Reset Option

Registered and non-registered policy holders are allowed up to two resets per policy year up to age 69. From age 70 to age 90, only one reset is allowed, and after age 90 no further resets can be made. The valuation date will be the date at which written notification of a request for a reset of the guarantee is received by NN Financial, and all resets trigger a new 10-year maturity period.

Purchase Options and Costs/Automatic Contribution Plan

The maximum issue age is 59 for registered policies and 90 for non-registered policies, and the minimum initial premium is $1,000 per fund. Subsequent lump-sum deposits may be made at a minimum $500 per fund, or through a pre-authorized payment service of a minimum $50 per fund each month. All additional deposits will mature 10 years from the next anniversary date. Funds are available for purchase on a back-end load basis only, based on a six-year schedule that declines from 6.00%. A multiple fund investment option is also available, subject to a $5,000 minimum credit balance per fund, where the policy holder may make automatic additional deposits and indicate the percentage to be invested in each fund.

There are no fees associated with the 75% policy guarantee, however, the 100% guarantee policy is charged a quarterly maintenance fee ranging from 0.06% to 0.22% per fund. For the underlying bond and equity funds, the current annual management fee is between 2.25% to 2.90% per fund.

Liquidity/Free-Redemption Criteria/Systematic Withdrawal Plan

Partial withdrawals may be requested at any time provided that the policy value is at least $500. Valuations will be based on current market on the date of written request and will not be guaranteed.

IMS III also has a Withdrawal Program in which minimum scheduled pay-out amounts are $80 monthly, or $200 quarterly, semi-annually, or annually. Contract owners of non-registered policies may withdraw up to 10.00% of net deposits every policy year, and RRIF/LIF policy holders are permitted regular withdrawals up to legislated annual minimums, without back-end load charges. This limit can be expressed differently as a monthly maximum of 0.83%, a quarterly maximum of 2.50%, or a semi-annual maximum of 5.00%. The value of all units will be based on current market values and each withdrawal will proportionately decrease the guarantee.

(Source: NN Financial, 1999)

Investment Fund Performance						
Fund Name	Fund Type	YTD	1 Year	3 Year	5 Year	10 Year
NN American Asset Allocation	GlBal	− 5.2	−	−	−	−
NN American Equity Index Fund	USEqt	− 3.2	−	−	−	−
NN Asset Allocation	CaAsA	3.1	13.1	10.5	11.4	8.7
NN Bond	CaBnd	− 3.3	− 1.5	6.9	9.2	9.0
NN CAN-AM	USEqt	2.6	24.1	19.7	20.6	−
NN CAN-DAQ 100	ScTec	28.8	73.6	−	−	−
NN Can-Asian	AsPac	29.6	50.7	− 1.6	2.0	−
NN Can-Emerge	EmgEq	14.6	33.9	− 9.5	−	−
NN Can-Euro	EurEq	3.0	22.2	19.8	−	−
NN Can-Global Bond	FgnBd	− 4.7	− 5.2	5.5	−	−
NN Canadian 35 Index Fund	CdnLC	12.8	29.1	12.1	11.5	6.9
NN Canadian Communications	Specl	18.1	−	−	−	−
NN Canadian Financial Services	Specl	− 16.0	−	−	−	−
NN Canadian Growth	CdnEq	3.1	17.3	9.5	9.2	6.3
NN Canadian Resources	NatRs	23.4	−	−	−	−
NN Canadian Small Cap	CdnSm	2.4	−	−	−	−
NN Dividend	CaDiv	0.8	6.6	7.5	10.0	−
NN Elite	GlBal	7.3	5.9	2.2	3.1	−
NN European Equity Index Fund	EurEq	− 8.9	−	−	−	−
NN Information Technology	ScTec	19.7	−	−	−	−
NN International Bond Index	FgnBd	− 13.5	−	−	−	−
NN International Brands	Specl	− 2.7	−	−	−	−
NN Money Market	CdnMM	3.3	4.5	3.9	4.7	−
NN T-Bill	CdnMM	2.6	3.6	3.0	3.7	5.3

(Source: BellCharts Inc., as of September 30, 1999)

North West Life APEX Funds

Descriptive Overview of the Insurance Company

North West Life Assurance Company of Canada
Ratings:
A (Excellent) — A.M. Best & Company
Passed all eight early warning solvency tests administered by TRAC Insurance Services Ltd.
Assets:
Over $12 billion as a member of the Industrial-Alliance Group of Companies

North West Life, a federally chartered Canadian financial services and insurance company based in Vancouver, British Columbia, is a subsidiary of Industrial-Alliance Life Assurance Company and a member of the Industrial-Alliance Group of Companies.

Investment Fund Managers
AGF Funds Inc.
Dundee Investment Management & Research Ltd.
Friends Ivory & Sime PLC
Industrial-Alliance Life Insurance Company

Death Benefit
In the event of the client's death, the beneficiary will receive the

greater of either the current market value of the contract or 100% of the total net deposits invested. Back-end load charges may apply.

Maturity Benefit

The maturity date for the policy must be selected between the 55th and the 69th birthdays of the client, and must be at least 10 years from the date of original investment. On the maturity date, the client will receive proceeds equal to the greater of either the current market value or the Minimum Maturity Value.

The Minimum Maturity Value is calculated at the market value exactly 10 years from the policy date, and is guaranteed to be at least 100% of the total original net deposits made before age 80 and before the 10 years prior to maturity. The guarantee level is 80% for subsequent deposits made during the final 10 years, and 75% for deposits after age 80.

At maturity, clients may choose to purchase an immediate life annuity, renew the contract, or withdraw the proceeds.

Guarantee Reset Option

Clients may request a reset of their Minimum Maturity Value at any time up to age 90. After age 80, resets will be calculated based on 75% of the current market value. All resets will trigger a new maturity date which is at least 10 years in duration.

Purchase Options and Costs/Automatic Contribution Plan

An initial investment of at least $100 is required or, with a pre-authorized contribution plan, a monthly minimum of $25 per fund. Non-registered and RRIF plans may be issued up to age 90, and for RRSPs and LIFs, up to the current age restriction as outlined by government legislation.

Transfers of a minimum $100 between investment funds are permitted at any time. All funds are available for purchase on a back-end load basis, based on a declining six-year schedule that begins at 6.00%. The current annual management fee is between 1.75% and 2.50% per fund.

Liquidity/Free-Redemption Criteria/Systematic Withdrawal Plan

The client may request in writing partial or full withdrawals of a minimum $250 per fund at any time. The remaining value of units must be at least $100 after redemption. A systematic withdrawal plan may be established if the contract has an accumulated value of $15,000 or more; payments must be a minimum of $100. All valuations will be based on current market, and will cause a proportionate reduction in the guarantees.

A Redemption Privilege allows investors to redeem up to 10.00% of the contract value without any back-end load charges, calculated as of the valuation date of the preceding year. RRIFs and LIFs are allowed redemptions of 20.00%. Any withdrawals beyond this amount, including SWPs, will be subject to any applicable back-end load charges.

(Source: North West Life, 1999)

Investment Fund Performance						
Fund Name	Fund Type	YTD	1 Year	3 Year	5 Year	10 Year
APEX Asian Pacific	AsPac	27.1	52.7	− 2.2	− 0.4	−
APEX Balanced (AGF)	CaAsA	1.2	10.4	3.7	6.0	6.3
APEX Balanced (Dynamic)	CaBal	18.7	24.8	−	−	−
APEX Canadian Growth (AGF)	CdnEq	4.4	23.3	3.6	7.1	5.6
APEX Canadian Stock	CdnEq	7.3	19.0	−	−	−
APEX Canadian Value (Dynamic)	CdnEq	6.3	10.5	−	−	−
APEX Fixed Income	CaBnd	− 1.1	0.0	5.6	7.6	9.4
APEX Global Equity	GloEq	− 4.2	14.7	−	−	−
APEX Growth & Income	CaBal	3.3	10.0	−	−	−
APEX Money Market	CdnMM	2.4	3.3	2.6	3.7	−
APEX Mortgage	CdnSB	− 0.3	0.3	2.7	−	−
APEX US Equity	USEqt	− 4.6	16.1	−	−	−

(Source: BellCharts Inc., as of September 30, 1999)

Royal & Sun Alliance Segregated Funds

Descriptive Overview of the Insurance Company

Royal & Sun Alliance Life Insurance Company of Canada
Ratings:
n/a
Assets:
$145.9 billion (as member of the Royal & Sun Alliance Insurance Group PLC)

The Royal & Sun Alliance Insurance Group PLC is one of the largest insurance groups in the world. Headquartered in the United Kingdom, with over 44,000 employees worldwide, the group transacts business in more than 130 countries by offering a broad portfolio of high quality life insurance, savings, investment, and retirement income products.

Investment Fund Manager
Royal & Sun Alliance Financial

Death Benefit
The beneficiary is guaranteed to receive, upon notification of the annuitant's death, 100% of all net deposits made (reduced proportionately by withdrawals) or the current market value of the policy, whichever is greater. No age restrictions are stated, and no back-end load charges will be applicable.

Maturity Benefit

At maturity, the client will receive the greater of either the current market value of the policy or 100% of total net deposits made. The maturity date is selected when the policy is first established, and it must be a minimum of 10 years from the issue date and a maximum of age 90 for non-registered policies. Registered policies are subject to existing age limits set by government guidelines. Clients have the option of taking the proceeds in cash, renewing the policy, or purchasing an immediate life annuity.

Guarantee Reset Option

No resets are available at this time.

Purchase Options and Costs/Automatic Contribution Plan

The minimum initial deposit is $500 per fund, or $50 under a pre-authorized contribution (PAC) plan; for RIF and/or LIF policies, the minimum is $7,500. Policies issued under a PAC plan must reach the minimum $500 value within the first 12 months. Non-registered policies may be issued up to age 85, and registered policies are subject to existing government age regulations (currently age 69). Subsequent deposits of at least $500 or $50 PAC will have the same policy maturity date, however, a new policy may have to be opened if deposits in excess of $100,000 are made in the five years prior to the maturity date.

Investment funds may be purchased on a no-load or back-end load basis, based on a declining six-year schedule that begins at 4.50% in the first year. The annual management fee currently ranges from approximately 1.50% to 2.00% for each fund.

Liquidity/Free-Redemption Criteria/Systematic Withdrawal Plan

The client may request a partial withdrawal in writing at any time before maturity, with valuations calculated at current market prices. Guarantees will decrease in proportion to each withdrawal. An Automatic Withdrawal Plan (AWP) may also be set up for non-registered policies with a value of $5,000 or more to provide for periodic cash payments.

For investment units purchased under the back-end load option, withdrawals of up to 10.00% for non-registered and/or RSP policies and 15.00% for RIF and/or LIF policies may be requested without incurring any applicable load charges, based on total deposits made as of December 31 of the preceding year. This provision is not cumulative and may not be carried forward.

(Source: Royal & Sun Alliance, 1999)

Investment Fund Performance						
Fund Name	Fund Type	YTD	1 Year	3 Year	5 Year	10 Year
Royal $US Money Market	FgnMM	3.0	4.1	4.4	4.4	–
Royal & SunAlliance Balanced	CaBal	2.7	8.3	9.0	9.9	–
Royal & SunAlliance Cdn Growth	CdnSm	17.4	22.5	1.8	–	–
Royal & SunAlliance Dividend	CaDiv	– 4.7	6.8	–	–	–
Royal & SunAlliance Equity	CdnLC	11.3	26.3	13.7	12.7	–
Royal & SunAlliance Globl EmMk	EmgEq	20.5	32.0	–	–	–
Royal & SunAlliance Income	CaBnd	– 1.8	– 0.5	6.3	8.5	–
Royal & SunAlliance Int'l Eqty	IntEq	8.5	27.8	13.2	–	–
Royal & SunAlliance Money Mkt	CdnMM	3.1	4.2	3.8	4.8	–
Royal & SunAlliance US Equity	USEqt	3.6	16.0	25.1	–	–

(Source: BellCharts Inc., as of September 30, 1999)

Standard Life Ideal Investment Funds

Descriptive Overview of the Insurance Company

Standard Life Assurance Company
Ratings:
AAA — Standard & Poor's
AAA — Moody's Investor Services
Assets:
$134 billion (worldwide)

With over 170 years of history in the insurance business, Standard Life was founded in Edinburgh, Scotland, in 1825. Standard Life has since earned a reputation of financial strength and security, and is Canada's only major financial institution with top ratings from two of the world's most prestigious rating agencies. It currently operates in Canada, the United Kingdom, Ireland, India, Spain, and Germany.

Investment Fund Manager
Standard Life Portfolio Management Ltd.

Death Benefit
The beneficiary is guaranteed 100% of all net deposits (including withdrawals, refunds, and transfers). At the time of the annuitant's death, the death benefit paid will be either the guarantee or the

market value. No age restrictions are stated, and no back-end load charges will be applicable.

Maturity Benefit
Clients are guaranteed 75% of net deposits (including withdrawals, refunds, and transfers), provided that the maturity period for the contract is at least 10 years and ends before the client reaches age 90 for non-registered contracts and age 69 for registered (RRSP) contracts. Proceeds may be received in cash, transferred into an annuity, or, for registered policies, transferred into a retirement income fund.

Guarantee Reset Option
No resets are available at this time.

Purchase Options and Costs/Automatic Contribution Plan
The minimum initial deposit for both non-registered contracts (no age restriction listed) and RRSP contracts (up to age 69) is $1,000 with a minimum of $250 per fund or a valid periodic automatic contribution agreement. RRIF contracts require at least $10,000 and $1,000 per fund. An automatic contribution of $50 per month or more may be set up, provided that the minimum deposit adds up to at least $250 in the first policy year. Subsequent deposits do not trigger new maturity dates.

Investment funds are purchased on a back-end load basis only, and the eight-year declining schedule begins at 3.50% in the first year. The management expense ratio is currently 2.00% for each fund, with the exception of the money market fund, which has an MER of 1.01%.

Liquidity/Free-Redemption Criteria/Systematic Withdrawal Plan
The client may request in writing a partial or full withdrawal of a minimum $250 per fund at any time before maturity. Guarantees do not apply and valuations are at current market prices. The policy guarantee amount will decrease in proportion to each withdrawal. No systematic withdrawal plans are available at this time.

Annual withdrawals of up to 10.00% of total back-end load fund units can be made in all accounts without any charges, provided the minimum balance is $25,000. RRIF/LIF contracts are allowed 20.00% of deposits in the first year and 20.00% of the book value at the beginning of the year for all subsequent years without back-end charges.

(Source: Standard Life, 1999)

Investment Fund Performance						
Fund Name	Fund Type	YTD	1 Year	3 Year	5 Year	10 Year
Standard Life Ideal Balanced	CaBal	1.7	11.4	10.4	11.3	9.7
Standard Life Ideal Bond	CaBnd	− 1.5	0.0	5.9	8.1	8.7
Standard Life Ideal Cdn Div	CaDiv	− 3.6	−	−	−	−
Standard Life Ideal Equity	CdnEq	11.2	27.4	14.6	15.4	10.6
Standard Life Ideal Int'l Eqty	IntEq	4.7		−	−	−
Standard Life Ideal Money Mkt	CdnMM	2.9	4.3	4.3	5.1	−
Standard Life Ideal Payout Bal	CaBal	− 2.2	−	−	−	−
Standard Life Ideal US Equity	USEqt	− 1.5	−	−	−	−

(Source: BellCharts Inc., as of September 30, 1999)

Sun Life SunWise 2000

Descriptive Overview of the Insurance Company

Sun Life Assurance Company of Canada
Ratings:
AA+ — Standard & Poor's
A+ (Superior) — A.M. Best & Company
Assets:
$375 billion

Headquartered in Switzerland, the Zurich Financial Services Group operates globally in more than 50 countries, with over 30 million customers worldwide. Its experience and credentials make it one of the world's largest and most respected providers of financial services.

Investment Fund Managers
AGF Management Ltd.
Fidelity Investments Canada Ltd.
Sceptre Mutual Funds
Spectrum United Mutual Funds Inc.
Trimark Investment Management Inc.

Death Benefit
Clients have the initial option of selecting a 75% or 100% death benefit guarantee; no subsequent switch between death guarantee

options is allowed. For the 100% option, the guarantee is at 80% only between the ages of 80 and 83 inclusive. Upon notification of the client's death, the beneficiary will receive the greatest of the market value of the contract, the value as of the last reset, or the guarantee amount of net original deposits, less any withdrawals and any applicable back-end load charges.

Maturity Benefit

At the 10-year maturity date, the client will receive an amount that is the greater of the current market value or the amount of the total net original deposit. All subsequent deposits will have the same maturity date under the same policy.

Guarantee Reset Option

The death benefit is automatically reset every year at current market value or at the existing guarantee amount, up to age 80. No resets are permitted for the maturity benefit.

Purchase Options and Costs/Automatic Contribution Plan

The minimum initial deposit is $1,000 to set up a contract. Subsequent deposits may be made at a minimum $250 lump-sum or $100 per month under a pre-authorized contribution plan. Non-registered policies may be issued up to age 80, and registered policies are subject to existing government age regulations.

Funds are available on a front-end load (0.00% to 6.00%) or back-end load option, based on a declining six-year schedule that begins at 5.50%. The management expense ratio ranges from 2.60% to 2.85% for most funds under the 75% death benefit guarantee option, and between 15 to 30 basis points higher for the 100% death benefit guarantee.

Liquidity/Free-Redemption Criteria/Systematic Withdrawal Plan

Partial withdrawals of at least $250 and/or $100 per fund may be requested in writing up to four times in a calendar year, subject to an administrative fee of $25. For requests in excess of the allowable 10% amount—calculated as of the contract's market value on

January 1 of the current year plus 10% of current year deposits — policies that have been purchased under the back-end load option will be subject to any applicable charges. The amount of the guarantees will decrease proportionate to each withdrawal.

A systematic withdrawal plan may be set up for non-registered policies at a minimum $100 per fund. The remaining policy value must also be at least $1,000 or $250 per fund. Registered policies such as RRIFs and LIFs are permitted withdrawals up to legislated annual minimums without applicable charges. All valuations will be at market value.

(Source: Sun Life Canada, 1999)

Investment Fund Performance						
Fund Name	Fund Type	YTD	1 Year	3 Year	5 Year	10 Year
AGF Amer Growth Class	USEqt	1.7	29.8	30.3	27.9	17.5
AGF Canadian Growth & Income	CaAsA	4.1	15.1	3.0	8.7	7.7
AGF Canadian Stock	CdnEq	6.7	23.7	10.3	9.2	7.6
Fidelity Cdn Asset Allocation	CaAsA	1.7	12.3	14.1	–	–
Fidelity Growth America	USEqt	– 0.7	19.3	20.3	20.9	–
Fidelity Int'l Portfolio	GloEq	1.8	21.6	18.6	15.9	12.7
Fidelity True North	CdnEq	5.0	23.7	13.3	–	–
Sceptre Balanced Growth	CaBal	– 2.8	2.0	6.2	10.6	9.3
Sceptre Bond	CaBnd	– 1.1	0.2	8.2	9.5	9.8
Sceptre Canadian Equity	CdnEq	1.8	12.4	–	–	–
Sceptre US Equity	USEqt	– 10.3	3.0	–	–	–
Spectrum United American Eq	USEqt	– 3.9	17.5	17.6	21.0	12.9
Spectrum United Cdn Bal Port	CaBal	1.6	11.3	7.2	9.7	9.3
Spectrum United Cdn Cons Port	CaBal	– 1.9	5.0	–	–	–
Spectrum United Cdn Equity	CdnLC	7.1	21.6	9.5	10.0	10.2
Spectrum United Cdn Grth Port	CaBal	3.0	14.9	–	–	–
Spectrum United Cdn Incom Port	CaBnd	– 2.8	1.4	–	–	–
Spectrum United Cdn Investment	CdnLC	0.2	10.3	12.5	12.9	7.0
Spectrum United Cdn Money Mkt	CdnMM	2.9	4.1	3.4	4.1	5.8
Spectrum United Cdn MxGrth Prt	CdnEq	4.4	18.5	–	–	–
Spectrum United Cdn Stock	CdnLC	1.6	15.7	9.4	9.5	6.3
Spectrum United Dividend	CaDiv	– 4.1	– 0.2	9.3	10.0	8.0
Spectrum United Glbl Equity	GloEq	– 2.6	17.6	14.4	11.7	–

Investment Fund Performance						
Fund Name	Fund Type	YTD	1 Year	3 Year	5 Year	10 Year
Spectrum United Glbl Gr Port	GloEq	4.7	21.0	–	–	–
Spectrum United Mid-Term Bond	CaBnd	– 2.1	– 0.5	5.7	8.0	8.5
Trimark Canadian Bond	CaBnd	– 0.8	0.7	6.6	–	–
Trimark Select Cdn Growth	CdnEq	16.7	19.6	8.5	8.5	–
Trimark Select Growth	GloEq	6.8	24.8	10.5	11.4	13.3

(Source: BellCharts Inc., as of September 30, 1999)

Because the SunWise 2000 funds were recently launched and do not have a measurable previous track record, the performance of the underlying **mutual funds** without the addition of insurance charges is used.

Talvest Synchrony Funds

Descriptive Overview of the Insurance Company

Maritime Life Assurance Company
Ratings:
A+ (Superior) — A.M. Best & Company
A1 — Moody's Investor Services
Assets:
$6.0 billion

Maritime Life was founded in Halifax, Nova Scotia, and incorporated in 1922. The company is organized into three product lines: group insurance, individual life, and investment products. In 1969, it was purchased by the John Hancock Mutual Life Insurance Company of Boston, one of the largest and most highly respected financial services companies in the United States, with a rating of A++ by A.M. Best & Company. It currently has approximately $100 billion U.S. in assets under administration.

Investment Fund Managers
Talvest Fund Management Inc., T.A.L. Investment Counsel
Van Berkom and Associates Inc.
Bank of Ireland Asset Management
Nicholas-Applegate Capital Management
John Hancock Mutual Life Insurance Company

Death Benefit

Deposits made up to age 76 are 100% guaranteed, after which the guarantee level drops by 5% each year until the age of 80, when the guarantee will remain fixed at 80%.

Any back-end load charges will apply on proceeds to the beneficiary, who will receive the greatest of the current market value, the policy value as of the last reset, or the guarantee amount.

Maturity Benefit

For all contracts of more than 10 years, the Stock Market Guarantee ensures that the amount received at the maturity date will be no less than 100% of the total deposits (less withdrawals) or the highest net asset value achieved on any given day prior to the final 10-year period of the contract. During the final 10-year term, the guarantee is 75% of the net deposits.

Guarantee Reset Option

During the time before the final 10-year period of a policy, the guarantee is locked in with automatic daily resets. No manual resets are available at this time.

Purchase Options and Costs/Automatic Contribution Plan

The minimum initial deposit is $500 for registered and non-registered accounts, and subsequent deposits must be at least $100, unless an automatic contribution plan is set up, in which case the minimum monthly contribution is $50. For non-registered plans, the total of all deposits made in the first year must be at least $5,000. The maturity date is fixed at the start of the policy, and is not affected by subsequent deposits.

All investment funds are available for purchase with a front-end load option, where the fee ranges from 0.00% to 5.00%, or a back-end load option which starts at 4.00 to 6.00% and declines 1.00% per year. The investment management fee for each Synchrony portfolio (selected by the client at the establishment of the contract) will range from 2.85% to 3.10% per year, which represents the total investment fee charged by all the underlying funds within the portfolio.

Liquidity/Free-Redemption Criteria/Systematic Withdrawal Plan

A systematic withdrawal plan is available for clients who wish to receive regular income from the contract, provided the total accumulated value exceeds $10,000. Clients may choose the amount and the frequency. A maximum 10.00% of the value of all back-end load option fund holdings — or, with RRIF/LIF policies, units up to the legislated annual minimum — may be withdrawn without incurring any charges. All values will be based on current market prices.
(Source: Talvest Fund Management Inc, 1999)

Investment Fund Performance						
Fund Name	Fund Type	YTD	1 Year	3 Year	5 Year	10 Year
Maritime Life Am Gr & Inc A&C	USEqt	-6.8	8.8	16.3	17.2	-
Maritime Life Bond A	CaBnd	-0.5	0.8	5.6	7.6	8.2
Maritime Life Discovery A & C	USSml	8.6	46.0	-	-	-
Maritime Life Divrsfd Eqty A&C	CdnEq	2.7	20.2	-	-	-
Maritime Life Money Market A	CdnMM	2.9	3.9	3.0	3.5	5.3
Talvest Cdn Equity Growth	CdnEq	9.5	26.7	-	-	-
Talvest Dividend	CaHln	-0.3	6.5	7.3	-	-
Talvest Foreign Pay Cdn Bond	FgnBd	-6.4	-4.8	7.0	8.1	-
Talvest Global Equity	GloEq	-3.3	16.9	-	-	-
Talvest Global Small Cap	GloEq	48.8	93.4	-	-	-
Talvest High Yield Bond	HiYld	4.7	4.6	-	-	-
Talvest Small Cap Cdn Eq	CdnSm	2.0	19.6	9.9	13.1	-

(Source: BellCharts Inc., as of September 30, 1999)

Because the Synchrony Funds were recently launched and do not have a measurable previous track record, the performance of the underlying **mutual funds** without the addition of insurance charges is used.

Templeton Guaranteed Investment Funds

Descriptive Overview of the Insurance Company

Allianz Life Insurance Company of North America
Ratings:
A+ (Superior) — A.M. Best & Company
Assets:
$19.1 billion U.S.

Allianz Life is a member of Allianz Group, one of the three largest insurance groups in the world. Headquartered in Munich, Germany, Allianz Group owns insurance and related companies in more than 50 countries and has more than 245,000 employees and representatives worldwide. Allianz Life originated in 1896 as North American Life and Casualty Company, and now sells accident, health, and life insurance throughout the United States and Canada with annual revenues exceeding $2.9 billion.

Investment Fund Manager
Templeton Management Limited, member of the Franklin Templeton Group.

Death Benefit
The death benefit guarantee ensures that beneficiaries will receive the greatest of the market value of the policy, the value as of the

last reset, or 100% of the principal investment (reduced proportionate to any withdrawals). This guarantee is unconditional, with no age restrictions. Back-end load charges will apply upon redemption, but the beneficiary will not receive any amount lower than the original investment. If the contract is renewed and transferred directly to the beneficiary, back-end load charges will not be applicable.

Maturity Benefit
Upon maturity at the end of 10 years, the client is entitled to receive the full market value, the value as of the last reset, or 100% of the original investment (less withdrawals), with no age restrictions. The contract is automatically renewed for another 10-year period unless the client requests a withdrawal of the investment. Mandatory maturity is age 100 for non-registered, RIF, LRIF, or Quebec LIF accounts, and age 80 for other LIF accounts. The maturity of RSPs, LIRAs, and LRSPs is at age 69, as legislated by government.

Guarantee Reset Option
Investors may lock in any investment gains by resetting the guaranteed amount up to four times per calendar year. Each reset will be made at current market value and will start a new policy period of 10 years. The reset option is subject to maximum age limits depending on the type of plan: age 90 for non-registered, RIF, LRIF, and Quebec LIF accounts; age 70 for other LIF accounts; and age 69 for RSPs, LIRAs, and LRSPs.

Purchase Options and Costs/Automatic Contribution Plan
The maximum age to establish a contract is 80 for non-registered, RIF, LRIF, and Quebec LIF accounts; 70 for other LIF accounts; and 69 for RSPs, LIRAs, and LRSPs. Initial purchases must be a minimum of $2,500, allocating at least $1,000 per fund. Minimum subsequent purchases are $500 per fund subject to a minimum contract-holding amount of $2,500.

With a minimum of $2,500 contract value, clients may set up an automatic contribution of at least $50. Each subsequent purchase on a particular date will have its own guarantee date. All funds are available for purchase on a front-end (0.00% to 6.00%) or back-end load basis. Only the Templeton Treasury Bill GIF is offered at no-load. Back-end fees begin at 6.00% and decline over seven years to 0.00%. The current annual management fee ranges from 1.85% to 2.40%, which includes insurance costs.

Liquidity/Free-Redemption Criteria/Systematic Withdrawal Plan
Partial withdrawals and fund switches must be made in increments of $500 or more, subject to the minimum contract value of $2,500. A systematic withdrawal plan can be started on a minimum contract value of $10,000, and each withdrawal must be at least $50. Any withdrawals will proportionately reduce the guarantee amount, and are based on fluctuating market values.

Withdrawals are subject to back-end load charges, if applicable, but clients are entitled to a maximum 10.00% annual withdrawal — based on the net value of any back-end load units purchased in the current year plus the market value of the units held on December 31 of the previous year — without any fees. RRIF/LIF policy holders are permitted, without charge, regular withdrawals valued at current market prices up to the legislated annual minimums.

(Source: Templeton Management Limited, 1999)

Investment Fund Performance						
Fund Name	Fund Type	YTD	1 Year	3 Year	5 Year	10 Year
Mutual Beacon	USEqt	− 2.5	10.9	–	–	–
Templeton Balanced	CaBal	5.8	13.1	11.0	10.4	–
Templeton Cdn Stock	CdnEq	6.0	15.1	9.9	9.7	6.4
Templeton Growth Fund, Ltd.	GloEq	9.1	20.0	12.0	11.4	12.3
Templeton Int'l Stock	IntEq	8.3	22.3	14.2	12.8	13.6
Templeton Treasury Bill	CdnMM	3.1	4.2	3.3	4.1	5.9

(Source: BellCharts Inc., as of September 30, 1999)

Because the Templeton GIF was recently launched and does not have a measurable previous track record, the performance of the underlying **mutual funds** without the addition of insurance charges is used.

Transamerica Growsafe

Descriptive Overview of the Insurance Company

Transamerica Life Insurance Company of Canada
Ratings:
A+ (Superior) — A.M. Best & Company
AA+ (Very High) — Duff & Phelps
Passed all eight early warning solvency tests administered by TRAC
Insurance Services Ltd.
Assets:
$2 billion, over $75 billion (Cdn) with parent company Transamerica Corp.
USA

The Transamerica Life Insurance Company of Canada is the wholly owned subsidiary of Transamerica Corporation USA, one of the world's largest financial service companies. Transamerica Corp. was originally incorporated in 1906 as the Occidental Life Insurance Company and later changed its name in 1942 to the Occidental Life Insurance Company of California.

A federal license in Canada was obtained in 1928 and the company was incorporated in 1970 pursuant to the Canadian and British Insurance Companies Act as Occidental Life Insurance Company of Canada. In 1983, following the lead of its parent company, Occidental became Transamerica Life Insurance Company of Canada.

With more than 90 years of history, Transamerica now operates through more than 6,000 financial advisors and provides a wide range of industry leading insurance and investment products.

Investment Fund Managers
Guardian Capital Inc.
Yield Management Group
Transamerica Investment Services, Inc.

Death Benefit
The beneficiary will receive, upon the death of the annuitant, the greatest of the market value, the value as of the last reset, or 100% of the principal guarantee, less reductions for withdrawals. Any applicable back-end load charges will be waived.

Maturity Benefit
The client will receive the greatest of the market value, the value as of the last reset, or 100% of the original deposits, less reductions for withdrawals. The term to maturity may be selected by the client, provided that it is at least 10 years. Deposits made in each of the five years leading up to maturity will be limited to 20% of the total guarantee amount of the entire contract at the beginning of the policy year.

Guarantee Reset Option
The Growsafe Freeze Option allows unlimited resets at any time. The maturity period will be extended a minimum of 10 years (or the term selected by the client) from the date of each reset.

Purchase Options and Costs/Automatic Contribution Plan
Transamerica Growsafe can be purchased up to age 90, with an initial lump sum of $1,000 or with pre-authorized contributions of at least $50 monthly. Any additional deposits will not affect the maturity date, but will be included in the guaranteed maturity/death benefit.

Funds are available on a back-end load option, based on a six-year declining schedule beginning at 6.00%, or on a no-load option with no redemption charges. Note that if redeemed within three months, no-load funds will be charged 1.00%. The management expense ratio ranges from 0.90% to 2.60% for each fund.

Liquidity/Free-Redemption Criteria/Systematic Withdrawal Plan
Periodic partial withdrawals and/or regular systematic withdrawals may be requested at any time. Valuations are based on current market prices and are subject to any applicable back-end load charges. Each withdrawal will proportionately decrease the guarantee.

Annual redemptions of back-end load fund units are allowed, up to 10% for non-registered accounts, and 20% for registered accounts (RRIFs/LIFs), without any applicable charges.
(Source: Transamerica, 1998)

Investment Fund Performance						
Fund Name	Fund Type	YTD	1 Year	3 Year	5 Year	10 Year
Trans Growsafe Cdn 60 Index Fd	CdnLC	–	–	–	–	–
Trans Growsafe Cdn Balanced	CaBal	16.4	28.5	11.6	10.8	–
Trans Growsafe Cdn Bond	CaBnd	– 2.3	– 1.2	4.8	6.2	–
Trans Growsafe Cdn Div & Inc	CaDiv	– 4.7	1.0	–	–	–
Trans Growsafe Cdn Equity	CdnEq	27.9	49.8	14.9	13.3	–
Trans Growsafe Cdn Money Mkt	CdnMM	2.9	4.0	3.4	3.7	–
Trans Growsafe Europe 100 Indx	EurEq	– 7.8	9.0	–	–	–
Trans Growsafe Int'l Balanced	GlBal	– 3.3	5.6	8.5	8.8	–
Trans Growsafe Japnse 225 Indx	JapEq	27.0	54.8	–	–	–
Trans Growsafe US 21st Centldx	ScTec	24.0	68.3	–	–	–
Trans Growsafe US 500 Index	USEqt	– 1.2	19.9	24.7	–	–
Trans Growsafe US Balanced	GlBal	–	–	–	–	–
Trans Growsafe US Bond	FgnBd	–	–	–	–	–
Trans Growsafe US Equity	USEqt	–	–	–	–	–

(Source: BellCharts Inc., as of September 30, 1999)

Trimark Segregated Funds

Descriptive Overview of the Insurance Company

AIG Life Insurance Company of Canada
Ratings:
AAA — Standard & Poor's
Aaa — Moody's Investor Services
A+ — A.M. Best & Company
Assets:
Over $165 Billion U.S. (AIG Inc.)

AIG Life Insurance Company of Canada is a federally chartered insurance company based in Toronto. It is a wholly owned subsidiary of American International Group Inc., a leading U.S.-based international insurance organization that underwrites commercial and industrial coverage in an extensive worldwide network of approximately 130 countries and jurisdictions. American International provides a range of financial services.

Investment Fund Manager
Trimark Investment Management Inc.

Death Benefit
Upon the death of the client, the beneficiary will receive the greatest of the market value of the contract, the value as of the last reset, or

the guarantee amount on original deposit, less any withdrawals and any applicable back-end load charges. The guarantee amount is 100% of net deposits made by the annuitant up to age 75, and 80% beyond and including age 75.

Maturity Benefit

The maturity guarantee is 100% for all deposits made at any age below 90, after which all deposits made will be guaranteed at only 80%. For LIF contracts, the 80% guarantee begins at age 70. At maturity, the policy is automatically reset for another 10-year term unless the client chooses to end the policy. The client would then receive the current value of the policy, the value as of the last reset, or the maturity guarantee (100% or 80% of the total value of all deposits less withdrawals), whichever is greatest. The date of maturity for the initial investment is 10 years after the policy date. Subsequent investments will mature either 10 years after the next reset or 10 years after the next anniversary date. Mandatory maturity is age 69 for RRSPs, 80 for LIFs, and 100 for non-registered plans, RIFs, LIFs, and LRIFs.

Guarantee Reset Option

Resets are allowed up to two times per year, and the maturity period of 10 years will be extended each time. After age 75, no further resets are allowed.

Purchase Options and Costs/Automatic Contribution Plan

The initial investment must be at least a $500 lump-sum deposit per contract, and subsequent deposits must be at least $100. Through the Trimark Regular Investment Plan, investors may invest as little as $30 with a choice of frequency from semi-monthly to annually. This regular deposit option is not available for RIF, LIF, or LRIF accounts. All deposits made within the same policy year will mature 10 years after the next anniversary date.

Investors may choose either a negotiable front-end sales charge (0.00% to 2.00% in Ontario and up to 4.00% in the rest of Canada) or a back-end load charge based on a six-year schedule starting at

4.50%. The management expense ratio ranges from 1.44% for fixed-income funds to between 2.77% and 3.75% for domestic and international equity funds.

Liquidity/Free-Redemption Criteria/Systematic Withdrawal Plan

Scheduled withdrawals are available for non-registered plans only, and the client has the flexibility to choose the amount and frequency of the payments. Partial withdrawals are calculated as a percentage of the current market value of the fund holdings, and the deposit guarantee is reduced by this percentage using the first in, first out (FIFO) method.

Up to 10.00% of back-end load units are redeemable per year without charges for all non-registered accounts. RRIF/LIF policies are permitted regular withdrawals up to legislated annual minimums without applicable charges. All valuations will be at current market prices.

(Source: Trimark Investment Management Inc., 1999)

Investment Fund Performance						
Fund Name	Fund Type	YTD	1 Year	3 Year	5 Year	10 Year
Trimark — The Americas	GloEq	− 0.4	17.4	1.5	3.2	−
Trimark Advantage Bond	HiYld	2.2	3.2	7.3	−	−
Trimark Canadian Bond	CaBnd	− 0.8	0.7	6.6	−	−
Trimark Canadian Resources	NatRs	27.5	22.9	−	−	−
Trimark Canadian Small Cos	CdnSm	8.9	9.4	−	−	−
Trimark Discovery	ScTec	36.5	76.9	24.4	−	−
Trimark Europlus	EurEq	25.1	28.0	−	−	−
Trimark Government Income	CdnSB	1.4	2.4	4.1	6.3	−
Trimark Indo– Pacific	AsPac	25.6	42.5	− 1.5	1.9	−
Trimark Interest	CdnMM	3.1	4.3	3.6	4.4	6.1
Trimark Select Balanced	CaBal	9.9	13.8	8.8	9.7	−
Trimark Select Cdn Growth	CdnEq	16.7	19.6	8.5	8.5	−
Trimark Select Growth	GloEq	6.8	24.8	10.5	11.4	13.3

(Source: BellCharts Inc., as of September 30, 1999)

Because the Trimark Segregated Funds were recently launched and do not have a measurable previous track record, the performance of the underlying **mutual funds** without the addition of insurance charges is used.

Zurich WealthGuard

Descriptive Overview of the Insurance Company

Zurich Life Insurance Company of Canada
Ratings:
AA+ — Standard & Poor's
A+ (Superior) — A.M. Best & Company
Assets:
$375 billion

Headquartered in Switzerland, the Zurich Financial Services Group operates globally in more than 50 countries, with over 30 million customers worldwide. Its experience and credentials make it one of the world's largest and most respected providers of financial services.

Investment Fund Managers
Zurich Investment Management
T.D. Asset Management Inc.
Scudder, Stevens & Clark of Canada Ltd.

Death Benefit
In the event of the death of the annuitant, the beneficiary will receive the greatest of the market value of the policy, the value as of the last reset, or the guaranteed amount of net original deposits,

less any withdrawals and any applicable back-end load charges. The guarantee level, for both reset value and original deposits, is at 100% if the annuitant dies before age 80, and at 75% on or after age 80. Any back-end load charges will not apply.

Maturity Benefit

Upon maturity after a minimum of 10 years, the annuitant may choose to renew the policy, purchase an annuity, or surrender the policy, and the value is guaranteed to be the greatest of the current market value, 75% of original net deposits made before age 79, or 75% of the value of the last reset, less any applicable surrender charges. All subsequent deposits made within the same policy year will share the same maturity date of 10 years after the last anniversary date. Non-registered policies will be transferred to an immediate life annuity after age 80, and registered policies will be subject to current government legislation.

Guarantee Reset Option

Resets are allowed up to two times per calendar year up to age 70, and once per year between the ages of 70 and 80. The maturity period of 10 years will be extended each time. No further resets are allowed after age 80.

Purchase Options and Costs/Automatic Contribution Plan

Policies may be issued up to age 80 for non-registered policies and up to the legislated age limit for RSPs/RIFs. The annuitant may elect to invest in any fund on a no-load or deferred-load option based on a six-year schedule, starting at 6.00%. For the first option, the initial deposit must be at least $10,000 or $500 per fund; for the deferred option, the initial deposit must be at least $500 per fund, or $50 per fund with a pre-authorized contribution plan. All subsequent deposits made within the same policy year will mature at the last anniversary date after 10 years.

The annual management fee for each fund ranges from 1.65% for fixed-income funds to between 2.20% and 2.80% for domestic and international equity funds.

Liquidity/Free-Redemption Criteria/Systematic Withdrawal Plan

Partial withdrawals may be requested in writing at any time. For requests in excess of an allowable 10.00% free amount, non-registered policies that have been purchased under the deferred-load option will be subject to any applicable surrender charges. The guarantee amount will decrease according to each withdrawal.

A systematic withdrawal plan may be set up for non-registered policies at a minimum $100 amount. The remaining policy value must also be at least $5,000. Registered policies such as RRIFs and LIFs are permitted withdrawals up to legislated annual minimums without applicable charges. All valuations will be at current market prices.

(Source: Zurich Investment Management Inc., 1999)

Investment Fund Performance					
Fund Name	Fund Type	1 Month	3 Month	6 Month	YTD
Zurich Balanced Index Fund	CaBal	1.5	3.0	5.0	–
Zurich Cdn 300 Eq Index Fund	CdnEq	– 1.7	1.4	8.6	–
Zurich Cdn Bond Index Fund	CaBnd	– 0.5	– 1.8	– 1.3	–
Zurich Int'l Equity Index Fund	GloEq	– 0.4	7.2	5.4	–
Zurich S-Term Investment Index	CdnMM	– 0.2	0.2	1.1	–

Fund Name	Fund Type	YTD	1 Year	3 Year	5 Year	10 Year
Scudder Canadian Equity	CdnEq	3.6	16.1	17.8	–	–
Scudder US Growth & Income	USEqt	– 5.0	6.2	15.5	–	–

(Source: BellCharts Inc., as of September 30, 1999)

The Zurich WealthGuard Funds were recently launched and therefore do not have a measurable previous track record beyond the six-month range. For the Zurich Scudder Funds, the performance of the underlying **mutual funds** without the addition of insurance charges are used.

Glossary of Terms

Anniversary Date: The date on which the contract/policy was purchased and an initial deposit was made.

Back-End Load: A sales charge applicable at the time of redemption of investment fund units, rather than at purchase (usually if held for less than seven or eight years). This is calculated on a declining basis, whereby the percentage fee levied decreases for each year that the fund units are held. Also commonly referred to as deferred sales charge (DSC).

Front-End Load: A sales charge levied at the time of purchase for investment funds, expressed as a percentage of purchase amount. There are no further charges applicable upon redemption.

Guarantee Reset Option: The option of locking in any capital gains and/or growth in the market value of a segregated fund contract. A new deposit amount would be established (when referring to death and maturity guarantees). The maturity date of the policy is usually extended for a new term.

LIF: Life Income Fund

LIRA: Locked-in Retirement (Savings) Account

LRIF: Locked-in Retirement Income Fund

Management Expense Ratio (MER): A measure of the cost of operating a fund, expressed as a percentage of average total assets. The MER should be distinguished from the annual management fee, because the MER includes the management fee or annual fee, charged by the fund manager, along with all marketing and administrative costs associated with the operation of the fund.

Maturity Date: The date on which the contract/policy expires, at which time the client may choose to renew or surrender the policy.

Policy: An investment made by an individual or other legal entity into a segregated fund, establishing a contract with a policy issuer.

RIF: Retirement Income Fund

RSP: Retirement Savings Plan

Surrender: To redeem or sell the units held in a fund.

Other personal finance books available from Stoddart Publishing

CHAND'S WORLD OF MUTUAL FUNDS
2000 Edition
Ranga Chand
ISBN 0-7737-6076-8 $22.95

Join the ranks of the Heavy Hitters. Make your mutual fund selections with an eye for bigger returns.

DIAMOND'S PROSPERITY GUIDE
A Passport to Wealth for Canadians
Ruby Diamond
ISBN 0-7737-6075-X $19.95
"It's time to take financial matters into your own hands," says Diamond. "If you don't, you'll never become wealthy."

THE POWER OF INDEX FUNDS
Canada's Best-Kept Investment Secret
Ted Cadsby, MBA, CFA
ISBN 0-7737-6083-0 $19.95
A new investment option with lower fees. This book shows you how to choose funds and allocate your assets for a solid, diversified financial plan.

VENTURING OFFSHORE
A Guide to Offshore Investing for Canadians
Sunny Handa, Danielle Miller, and Richard Smith
ISBN 0-7737-6063-6 $22.95
Finally, an inexpensive — and readable! — guide to offshore tax planning. This timely and much needed book covers all the essentials.

BEYOND MUTUAL FUNDS
Your Guide to Wrap Accounts
Larry Herscu and David E. Edey
ISBN 0-7737-6101-2 $22.95
The only book of its kind for investors who want more out of their broker than high fees.

A WOMAN OF INDEPENDENT MEANS
A Woman's Guide to Full Financial Security
Gail Vaz-Oxlade
ISBN 0-7737-3185-7 $32.95
This bestselling author zeroes in on the choices women have to make about cash and credit management, budgeting, retirement, and educational savings.

THE MONEY ADVISER
Second revised paperback edition
Bruce Cohen with Alyssa Diamond
ISBN 0-7737-6018-0 $24.95
"I'm tipping The Money Adviser *as the natural succcessor to* The Wealthy Barber *. . . a classic compendium."*
— *Michael Kane,* Vancouver Sun

50 TAX-SMART INVESTING STRATEGIES
Revised and updated
Kurt Rosentreter
ISBN 0-7737-6096-2 $22.95

Tax planning made profitable: Kurt Rosentreter has saved Canadians thousands of dollars by maximizing their after-tax cash flows.

THE PIG AND THE PYTHON
How to Prosper from the Aging Baby Boom
David Cork with Susan Lightstone
ISBN 0-7737-5827-5 $16.95

Why you should be in the stock market!
Over 80,000 copies sold!

WHEN THE PIG GOES TO MARKET
How to Acheive Long-Term Investing Success
David Cork with Susan Lightstone
ISBN 0-7737-6025-3 $19.95

How you should invest in the market. Further guidance on economic prosperity!

MONEY LOGIC
Financial Planning for the Smart Investor
Moshe A. Milevsky, Ph.D., with Michael Posner
ISBN 0-7737-3171-7 $28.95

Professor Milevsky's groundbreaking ideas on money and markets take the risk out of investing.

For more on these and other Stoddart books, visit our web site: www.genpub.com/stoddart